Flowers on the Far Side

Acknowledgements and credits

I am grateful to my mother, wife and daughter for their incredible support and motivation behind this work. Fortunate to have an artistic eye right at home to critique and guide along the way.

Secondly, I am immensely grateful to all the brilliant artists and digital creators on Canva for making creativity so fluid. Sky is the limit!

The use of Canva fonts and elements are subject to Clause 5 of Canva's Content License Agreement as a paid subsribed user of Canva.com

This publication designed in Affinity Publisher as a paid subscriber.

I am a hobby writer that takes pride in writing poetry and prose in particular. An avid learner from mother nature and many of her facets.

Readers are encouraged to follow my Instagram handle - @WordyVirdee - for musings and nature moments. All pictures are my own captures (unless otherwise noted).

Blessings!

TABLE OF CONTENTS

WINGS & FLOWERS

Pages 4 - 23

NATURE & BIRDS

Pages 44 - 63

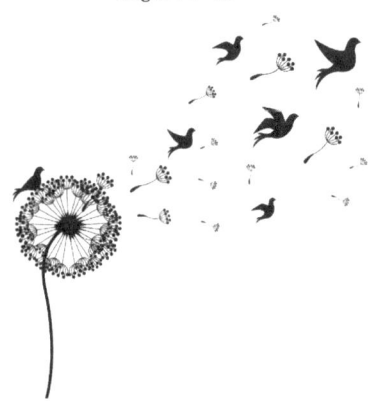

MOON & STARS

Pages 24 - 43

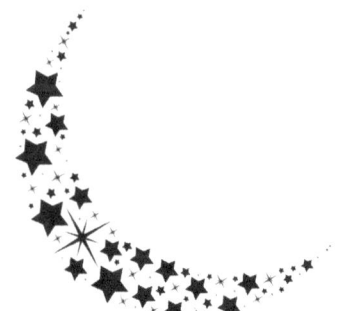

LOVE & LIFE

Pages 64 - 99

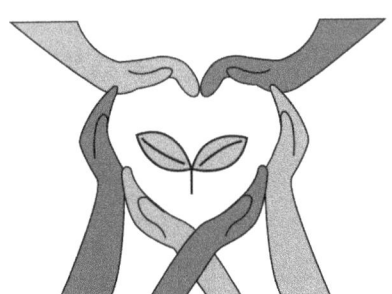

A butterfly suddenly wavered by,
As I casually looked out the window.
Its flight was erratic but elegant,
Its appearancce pretty, yet majestic.
I desired to chase it, to its destination,
But froze in my very stance instead.
Cherishing its being and presence,
Energized by the ether and hot sun.
It seemed in a hurry, beating its wings,
I wish it would stay, dance little longer.
Its journey carried it away, somewhere.
Hopes, wishes, desires, circle around,
Yet life, like that butterfly, flies away

A butterfly suddenly wavered by,
As I casually looked out the window.
Its flight was erratic but elegant,
Its appearance pretty, yet majestic.
I desired to chase it to its destination,
But froze in my very stance instead.
Cherishing its being and presence,
Energized by the ether and hot sun.
It seemed in a hurry, beating its wings,
I wish it would stay, dance little longer.
Its journey carried it away, somewhere.
Hopes, wishes, desires, circle around,
Yet life, like that butterfly, flies away!

Wordy Virdee

On a warm, bright, sunny, calm day!
Quick quirky storm caused a panic.
Little delicate flowers hit by mighty hail,
Birds utterly frightened, losing nests.
Trees had just blossomed in spring,
Parted ways with the colourful leaves.
Gale winds uprooting them from earth,
As they'd just enlivened from cold winter.
Such is the iffy balance of life, by nature,
Some birds suffered destruction of abode,
While others delighted after it all passed.
Plentiful worms over-filled their tiny beaks,
Exposed by sodden earth pelted by rain.
This too shall pass, while mystery remains!

WordyVirdee

On a warm, bright, sunny, calm day!
Quick quirky storm caused a panic.
Little delicate flowers hit by mighty hail,
Birds utterly frightened, losing nests.
Trees had just blossomed in spring,
Parted ways with the colourful leaves.
Gale winds uprooting them from earth,
As they'd just enlivened from cold winter.
Such is the iffy balance of life, by nature,
Some birds suffered destruction of abode,
While others delighted after it all passed.
Plentiful worms over-filled their tiny beaks,
Exposed by sodden earth pelted by rain.
This too shall pass, while mystery remains.

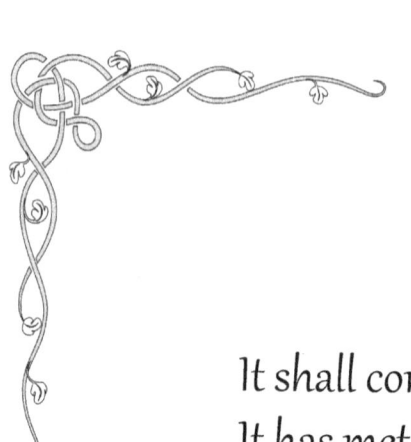

It shall come to us all,
It has met all before us,
It indiscriminates, it has,
No algorithms, no plans.
Death. Strike it will, kill,
Us all. But the pain cuts,
Deep, when it's a child.
Fighting to stay alive,
Every breath she battled,
To keep her flame alight.
Rest in peace beautiful little,
Child. Your pain ends, we'll,
Carry it forever in our hearts!
.

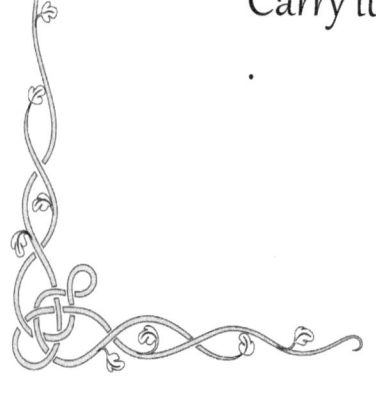

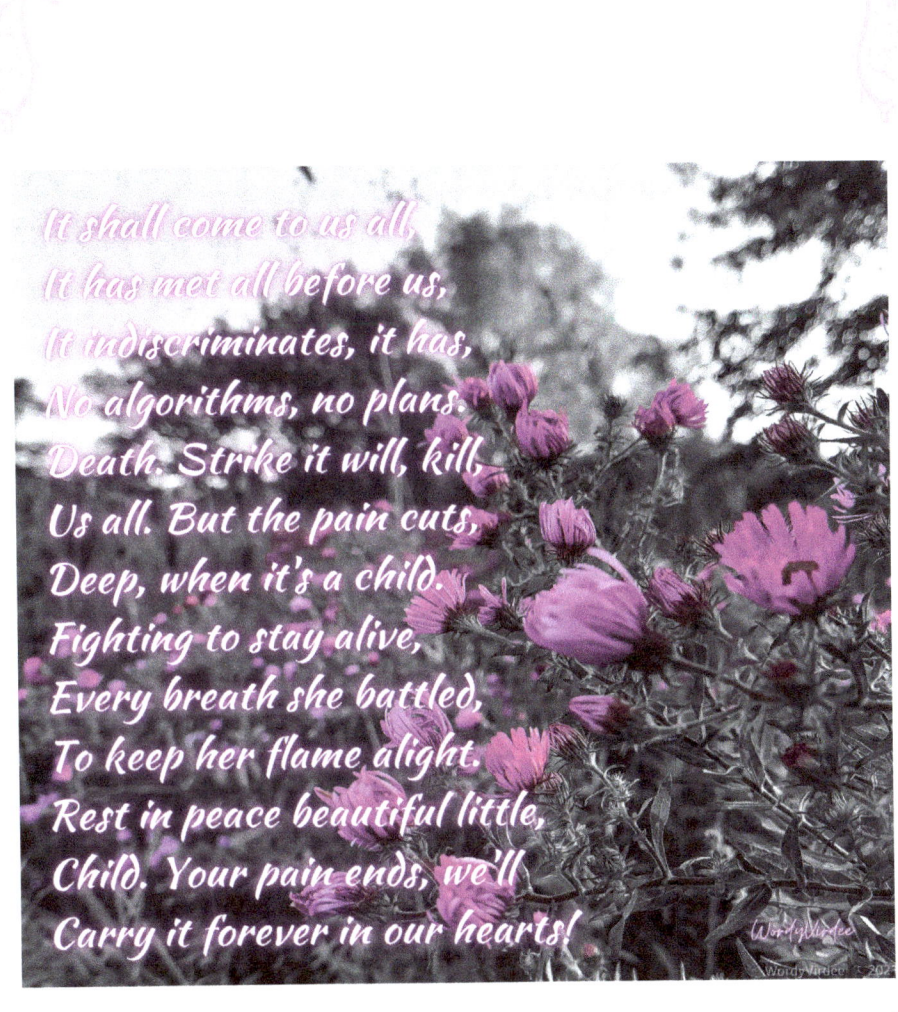

It shall come to us all,
It has met all before us,
It indiscriminates, it has,
No algorithms, no plans.
Death. Strike it will, kill,
Us all. But the pain cuts,
Deep, when it's a child.
Fighting to stay alive,
Every breath she battled,
To keep her flame alight.
Rest in peace beautiful little,
Child. Your pain ends, we'll
Carry it forever in our hearts!

The deepest part of the roots,
Remain buried forever; in the,
Dark of the cold earthly ground.
Yet they feel the shine of distant
Stars, by virtue of highest twigs,
Outstretched, frolicking in wind,
Cajoling glistening orbs up above,
Nature's own remarkable concert;
Par excellence, to entertain itself!

Wardy Virdee

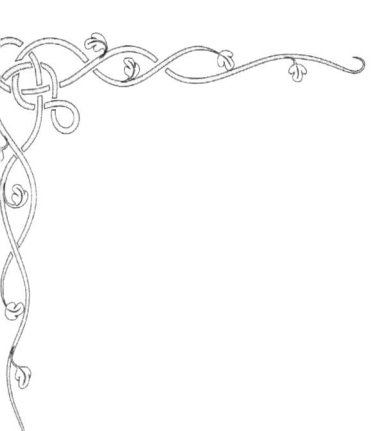
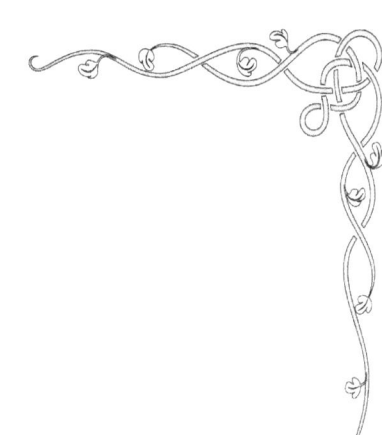

The deepest part of the roots,
Remain buried forever; in the
Dark of the cold earthly ground.
Yet they feel the shine of distant
Stars, by virtue of highest twigs,
Outstretched, frolicking in wind,
Cajoling glistening orbs up above,
Nature's own remarkable concert;
Par excellence, to entertain itself!

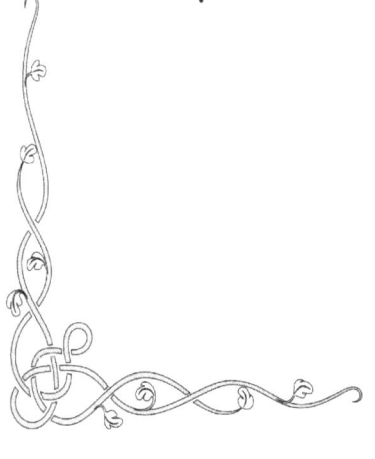
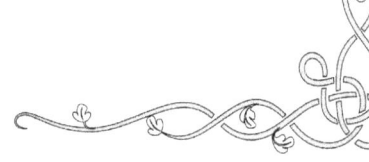

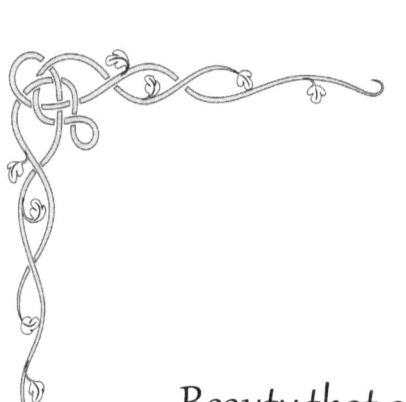
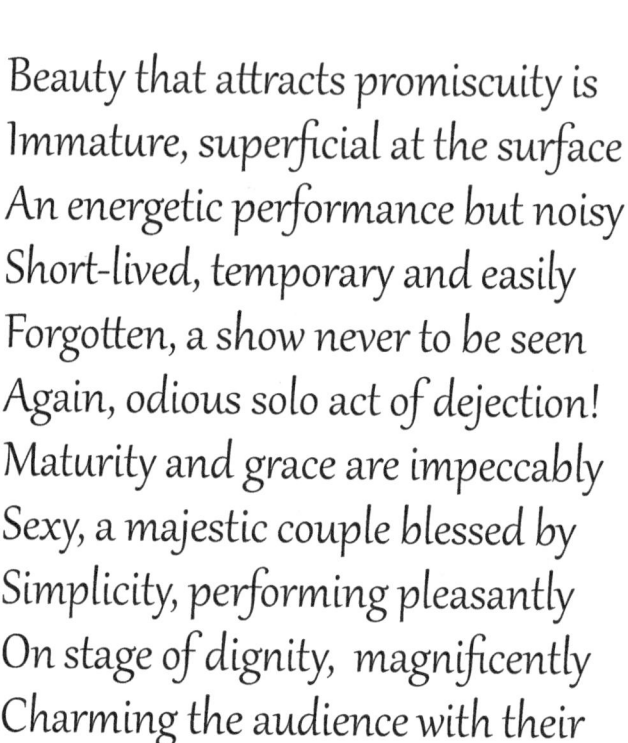

Beauty that attracts promiscuity is
Immature, superficial at the surface
An energetic performance but noisy
Short-lived, temporary and easily
Forgotten, a show never to be seen
Again, odious solo act of dejection!
Maturity and grace are impeccably
Sexy, a majestic couple blessed by
Simplicity, performing pleasantly
On stage of dignity, magnificently
Charming the audience with their
Utmost charm, nobility and honor!
.

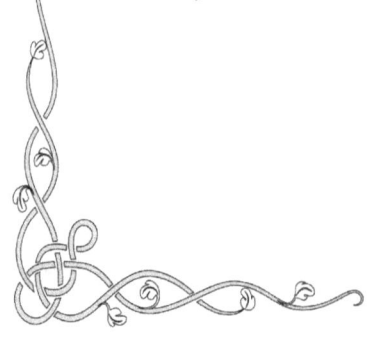

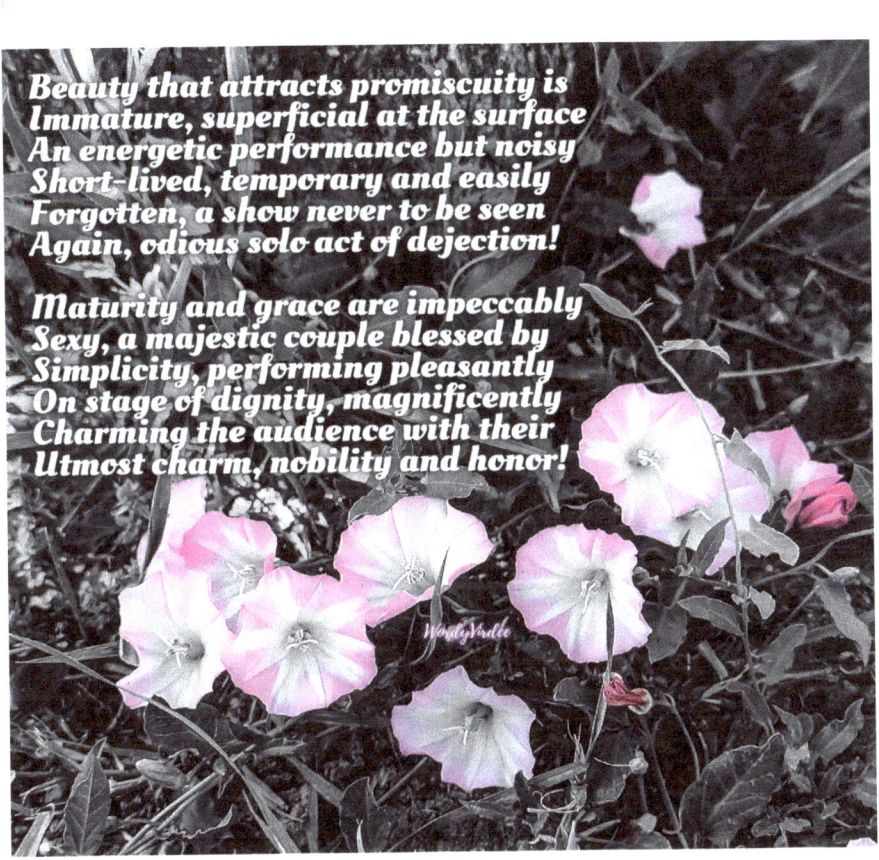

Beauty that attracts promiscuity is
Immature, superficial at the surface
An energetic performance but noisy
Short-lived, temporary and easily
Forgotten, a show never to be seen
Again, odious solo act of dejection!

Maturity and grace are impeccably
Sexy, a majestic couple blessed by
Simplicity, performing pleasantly
On stage of dignity, magnificently
Charming the audience with their
Utmost charm, nobility and honor!

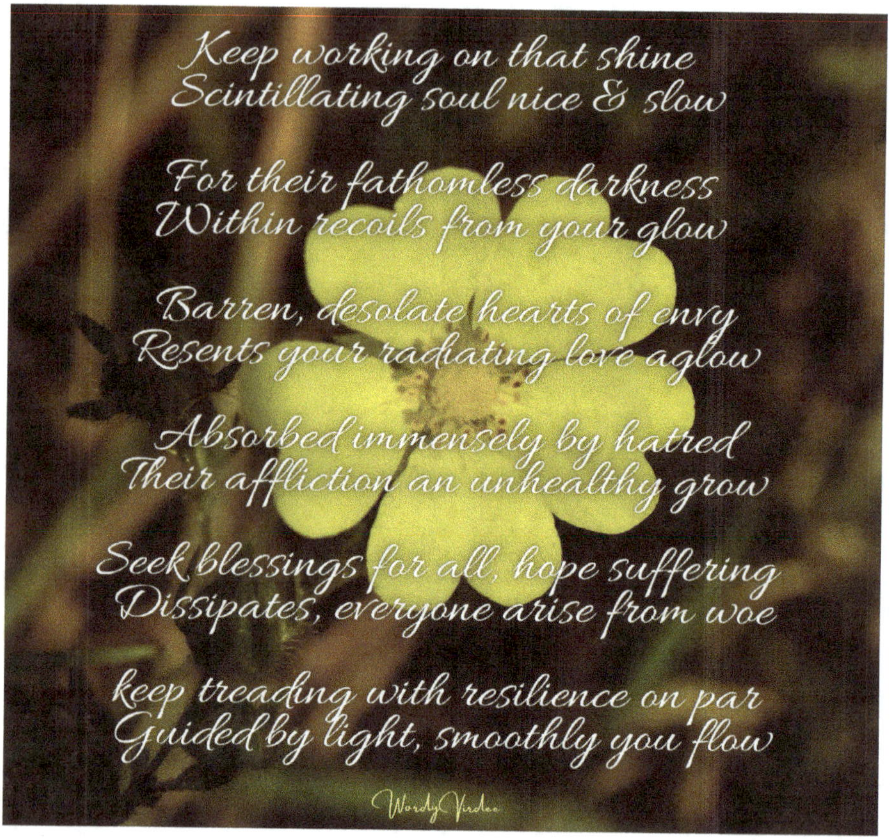

Keep working on that shine
Scintillating soul nice & slow

For their fathomless darkness
Within recoils from your glow

Barren, desolate hearts of envy
Resents your radiating love aglow

Absorbed immensely by hatred
Their affliction an unhealthy grow

Seek blessings for all, hope suffering
Dissipates, everyone arise from woe

keep treading with resilience on par
Guided by light, smoothly you flow

Wordy Virdee

Keep working on that shine
Scintillating soul nice & slow

For their fathomless darkness
Within, recoils from your glow

Barren, desolate hearts of envy
Resents your radiating love aglow

Absorbed immensely by hatred
Their affliction an unhealthy grow

Seek blessings for all, hope suffering
Dissipates, everyone arise from woe

Keep treading with resilience on par
Guided by light, smoothly you flow

.

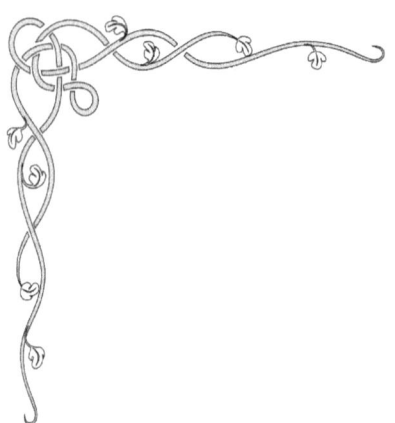
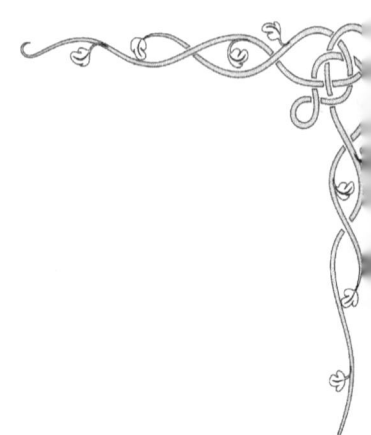

Cherish beautiful flowers at all
Opportunities presented to you,
They buzz your soul ever so high!

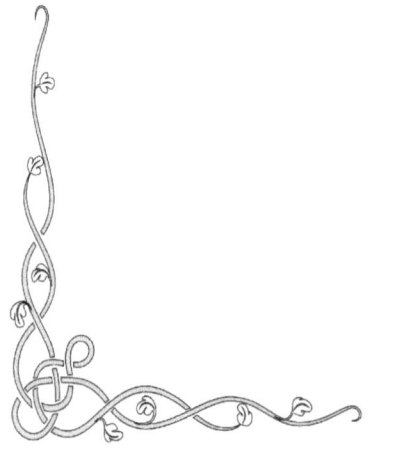
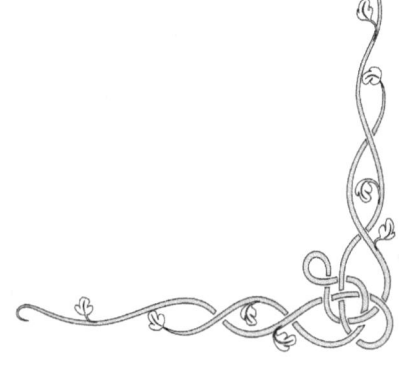

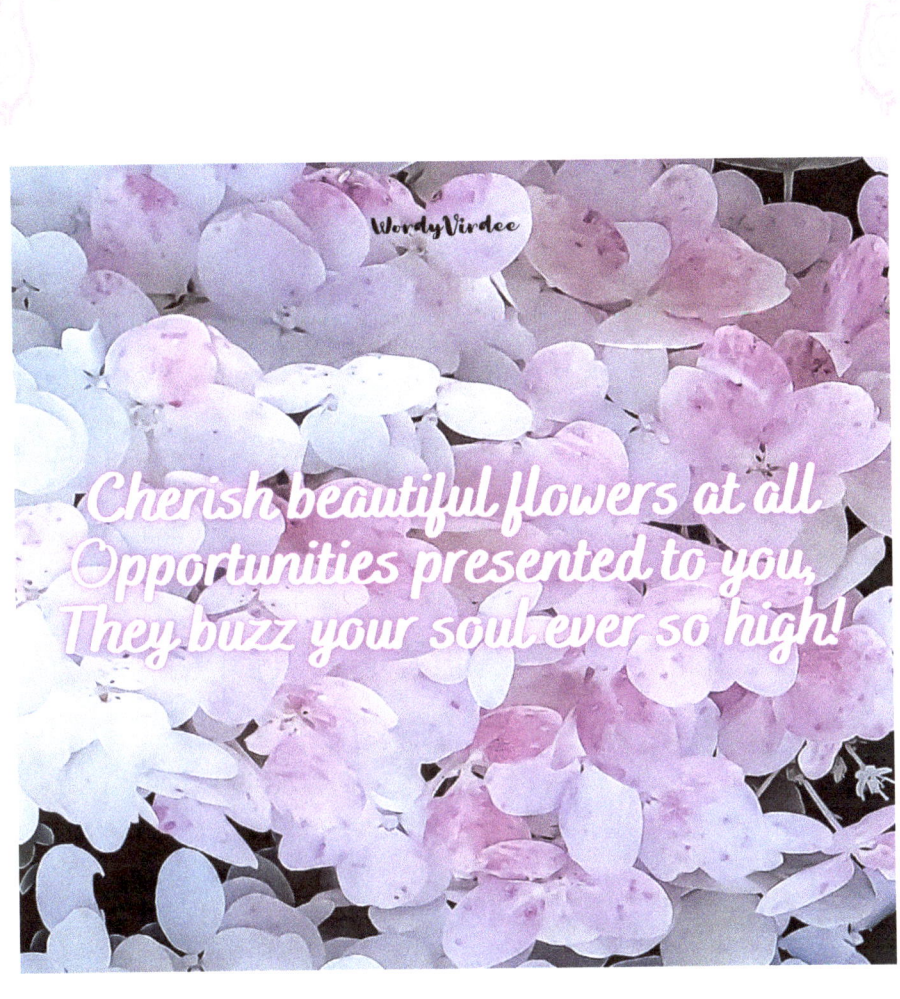

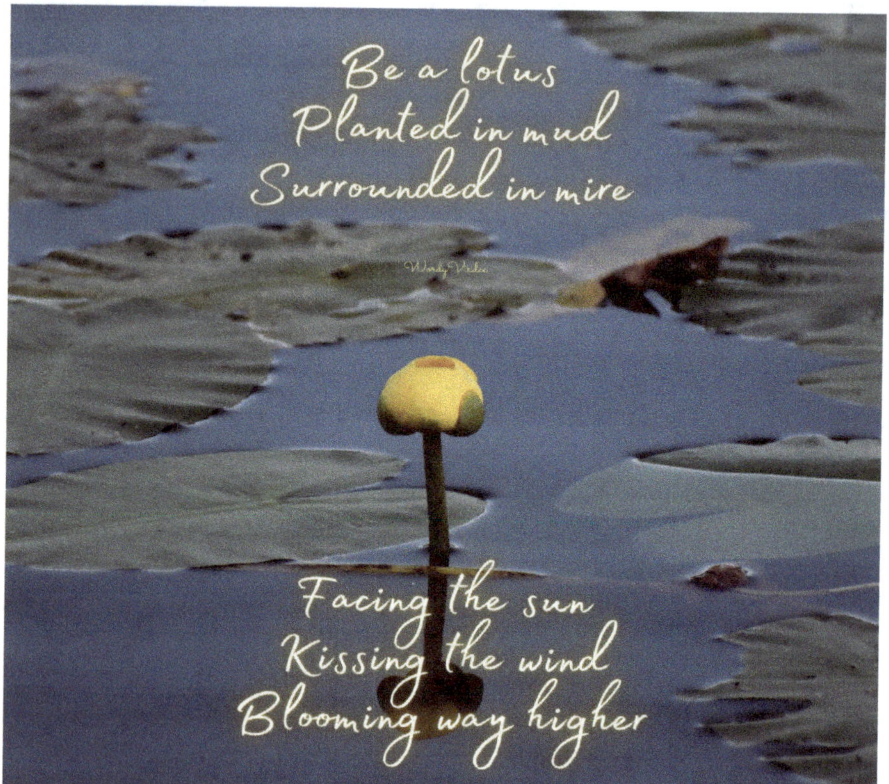

> Be a lotus
> Planted in mud
> Surrounded in mire
>
> Facing the sun
> Kissing the wind
> Blooming way higher

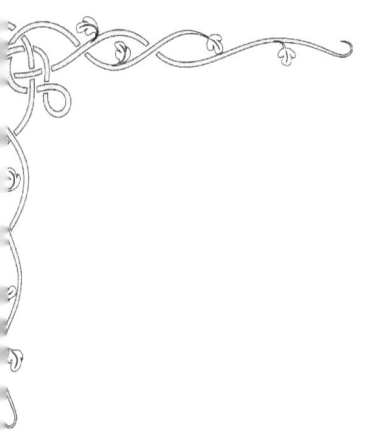
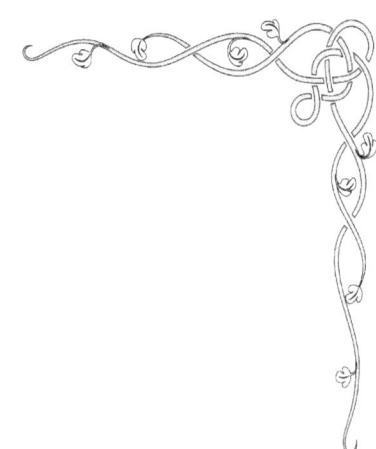

Be a lotus
Planted in mud
Surrounded in mire
Facing the sun
Kissing the wind
Blooming way higher

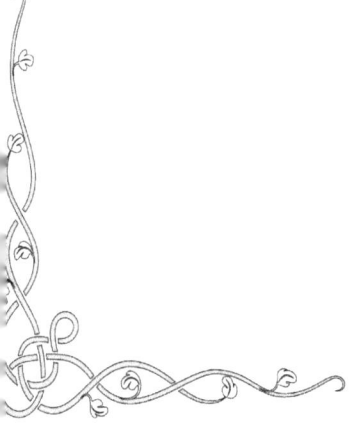
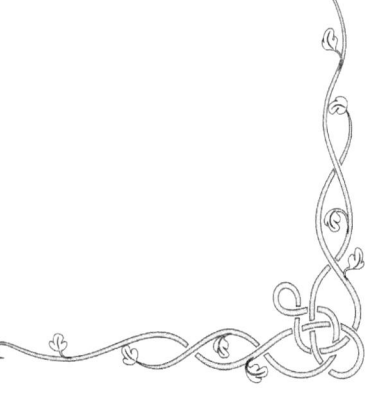

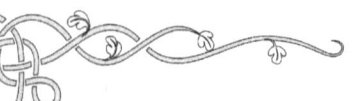
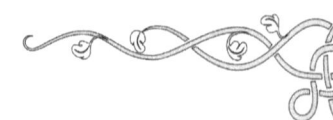

A lesson these wildflowers gave me
While trekking in the forest, seeking
The inner depths, the beauty inside

Grow confidently, to your full potential
Without any intervention, on your own
Where it suits you, to leave your mark

Let them travel to you for the beauty
You possess, the charm that attracts
While you remain rooted deep and strong

The common planted flowers surely entice
The gardeners, and the passers-by alike
But they get pruned, cultivated and priced

So be like a wildflower flourishing, where
It is in your power to prosper, at your will
Of your own accord, without conditioning

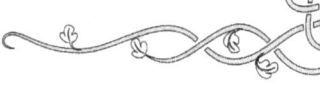

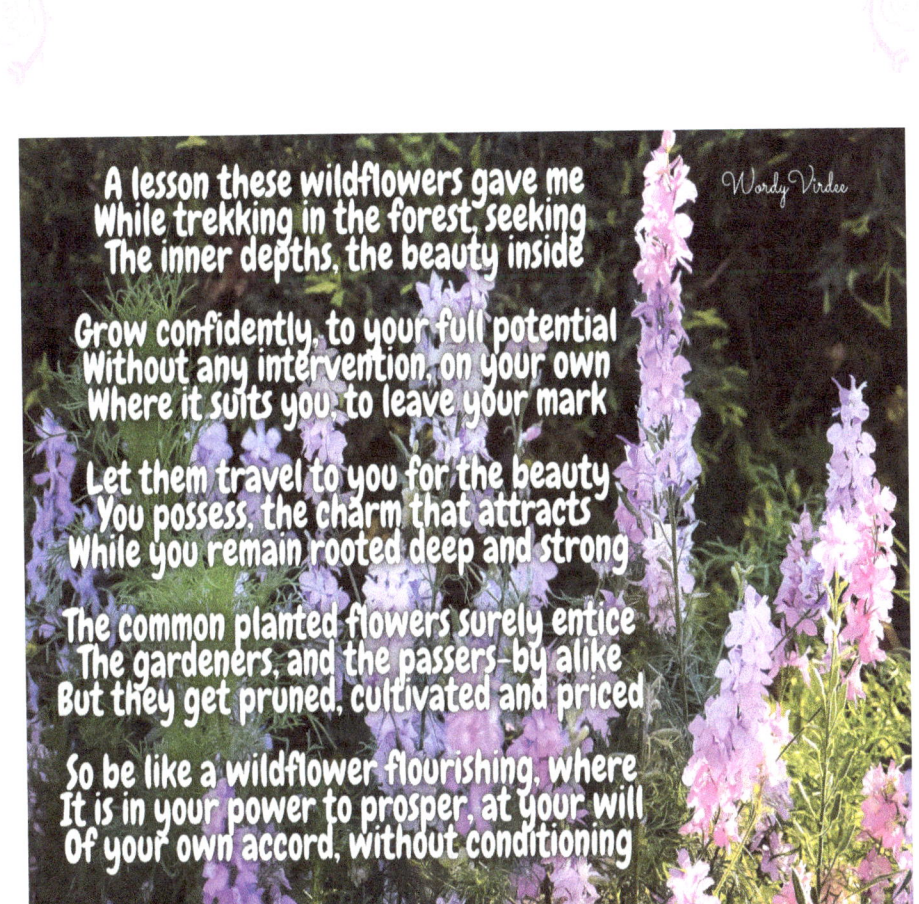

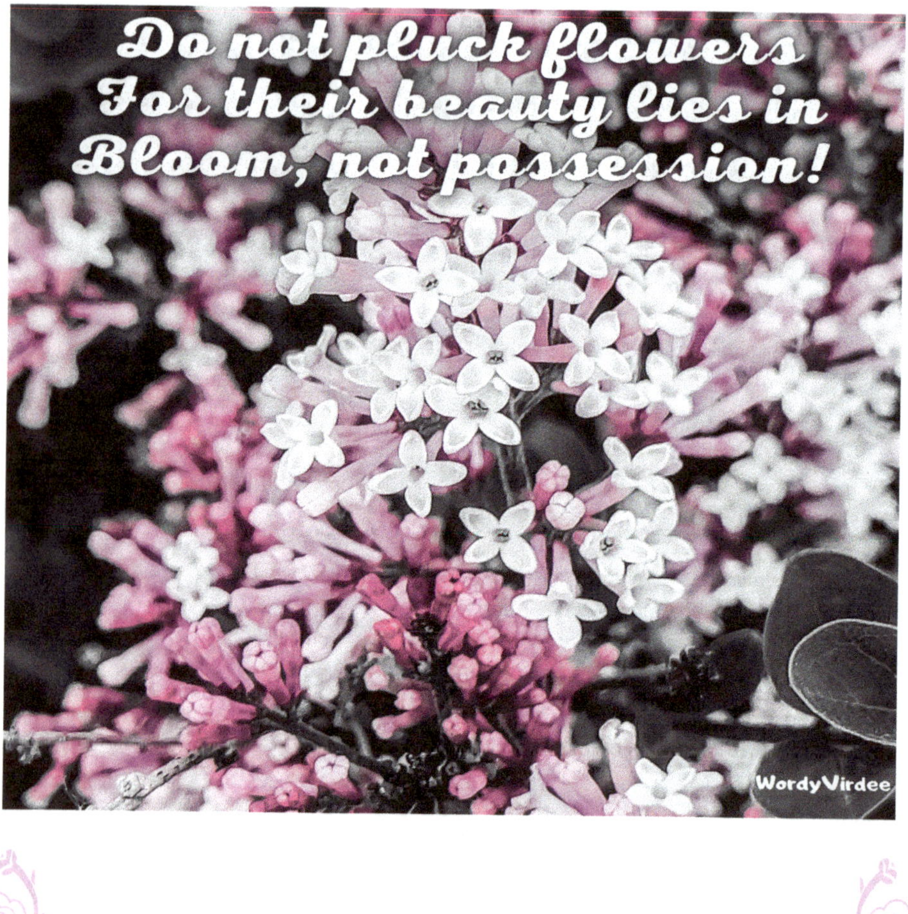

> *Do not pluck flowers*
> *For their beauty lies in*
> *Bloom, not possession!*

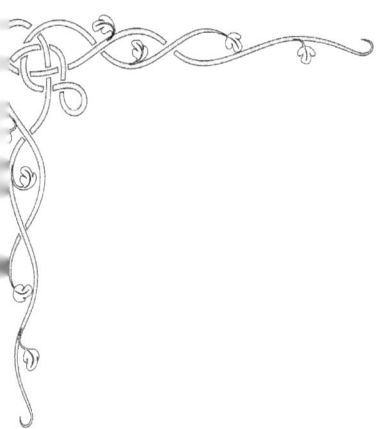
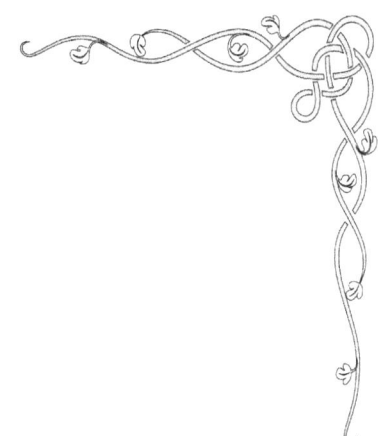

Do not pluck flowers
For their beauty lies in
Bloom, not possession!

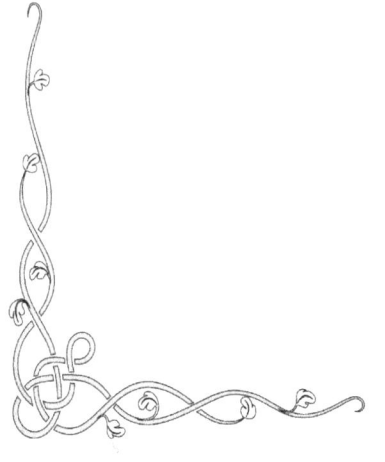
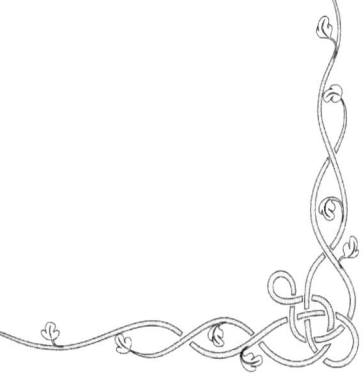

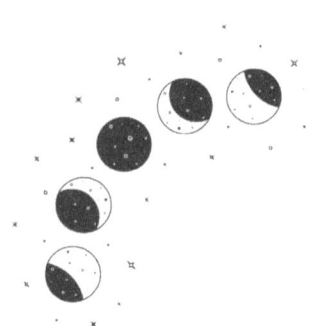

For some, the moon travels
Charting through their zodiac.
For me, moon fondly paces,
Magically through my heart.

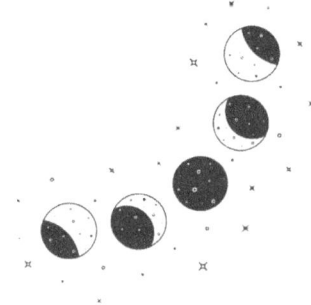

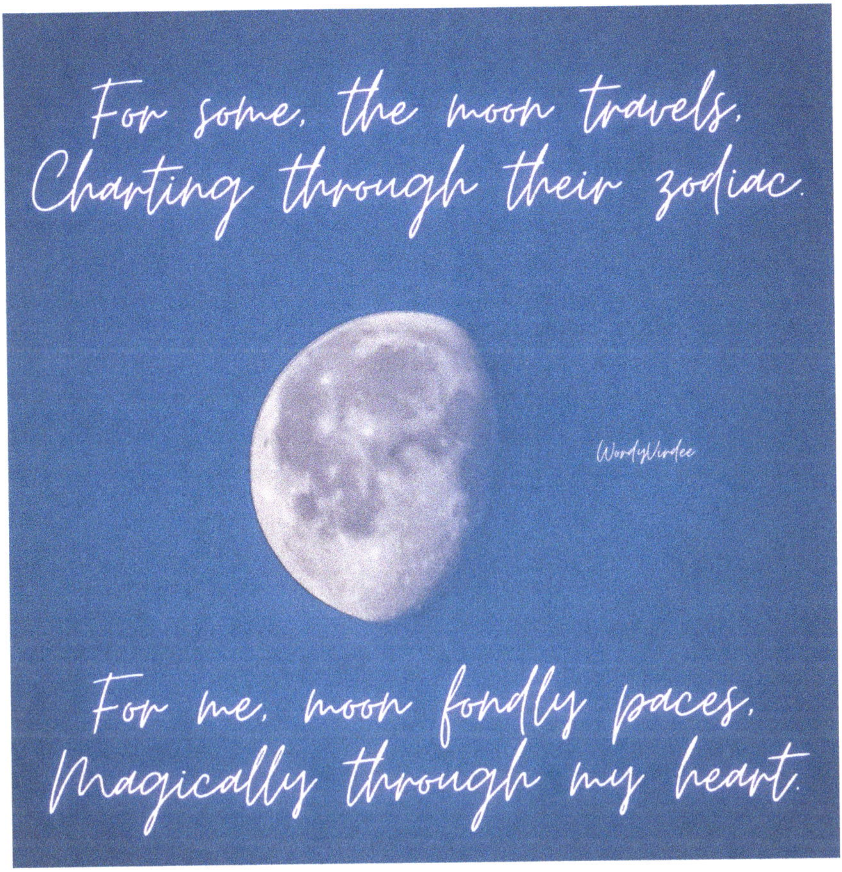

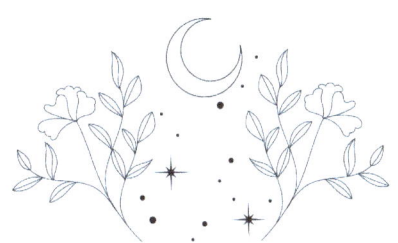

For some, the moon travels,
Charting through their zodiac.

For me, moon fondly paces,
Magically through my heart.

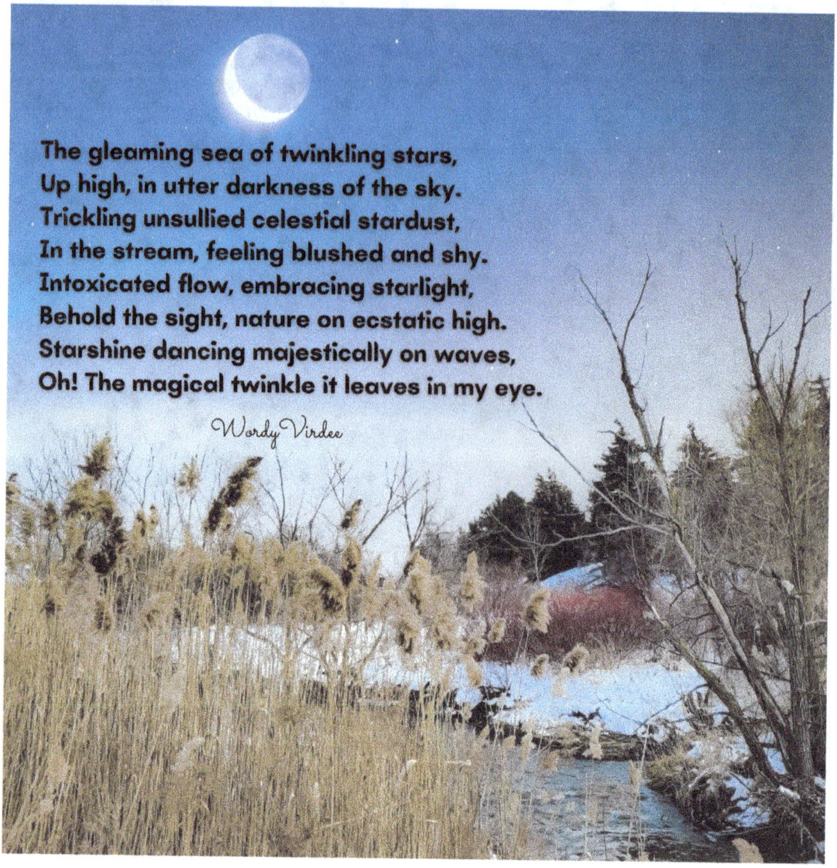

The gleaming sea of twinkling stars,
Up high, in utter darkness of the sky.
Trickling unsullied celestial stardust,
In the stream, feeling blushed and shy.
Intoxicated flow, embracing starlight,
Behold the sight, nature on ecstatic high.
Starshine dancing majestically on waves,
Oh! The magical twinkle it leaves in my eye.

Wordy Virdee

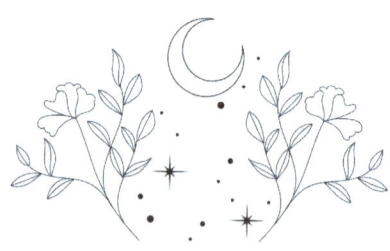

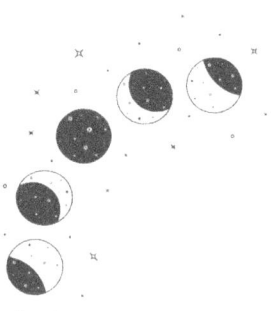

The gleaming sea of twinkling stars,
Up high, in utter darkness of the sky.
Trickling unsullied celestial stardust,
In the stream, feeling blushed and shy.
Intoxicated flow, embracing starlight,
Behold the sight, nature on ecstatic high.
Starshine dancing majestically on waves,
Oh! The magical twinkle it leaves in my eye.

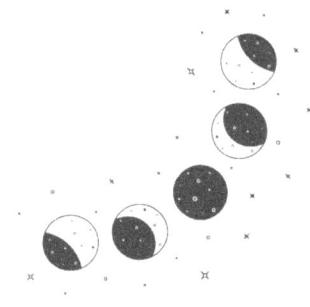

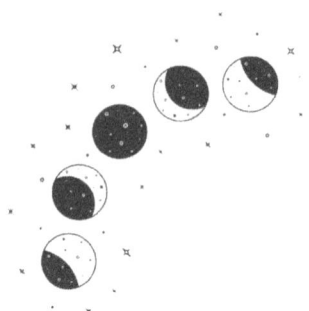

If you can't shine yourself,
Then just be there to reflect.
The light of someone; who can,
Either way, you're a beacon!

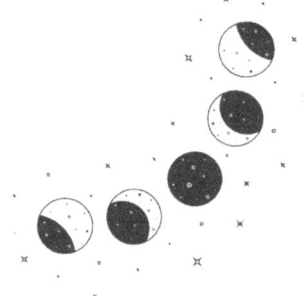

If you can't shine yourself,
Then just be there, to reflect.

The light of someone; who can,
Either way, you're a beacon!

Wendy Virden

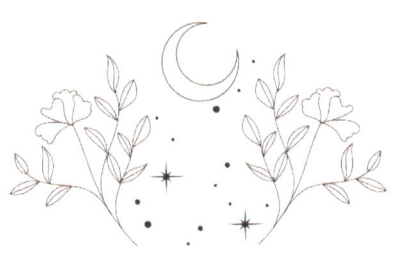

Moon is full tonight
A disk glowing white
In the sky at a height
Stars twinkling bright
Bonny sparkles of light
Behold the nightly sight
As it sets the soul right
Fascination takes flight
Beloved by side held tight
Imploring love to full might
In awe of divine nature I write

& ✒ @WordyVirdee

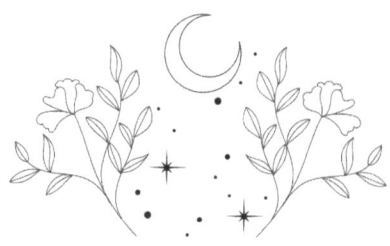

Moon is full tonight
A disk glowing white
In the sky at a height
Stars twinkling bright
Bonny sparkles of light
Behold the nightly sight
As it sets the soul right
Fascination takes flight
Beloved by side held tight
Imploring love to full might
In awe of divine nature I write

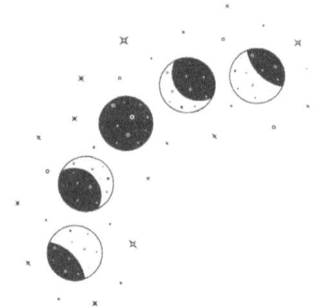

Twinkling stars up above in the sky
Some yonder others perched up high
Some gleaming bright, others a little shy
Shining their light, reaching down each eye
Burning constantly hot, yet soothingly gratify

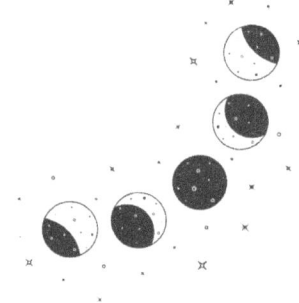

Twinkling stars up above in the sky
Some yonder others perched up high
Some gleaming bright, others a little shy
Shining their light, reaching down each eye
Burning constantly hot, yet soothingly gratify

Comparing her beauty tonight
With moon when it rose in sight

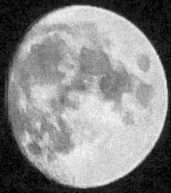

Gleaming graciously bright white
Darling! You took away it's delight

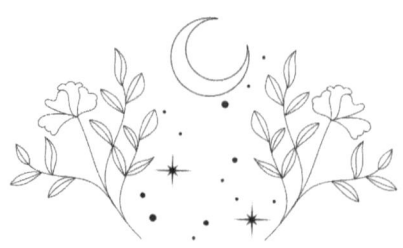

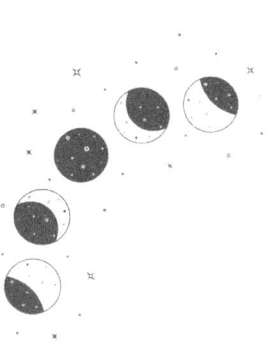

Comparing her beauty tonight
With moon when it rose in sight
Gleaming graciously bright white
Darling! You took away its delight

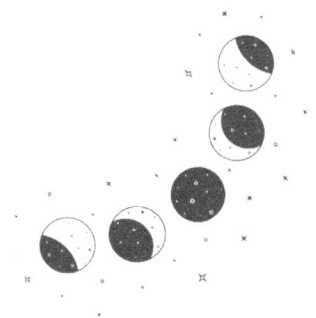

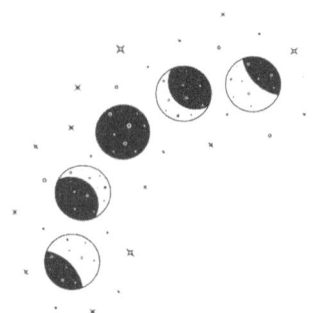

Not every load you carry is painful
Some are majestical and beautiful

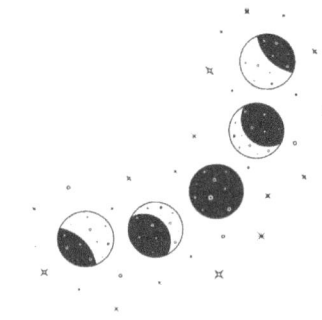

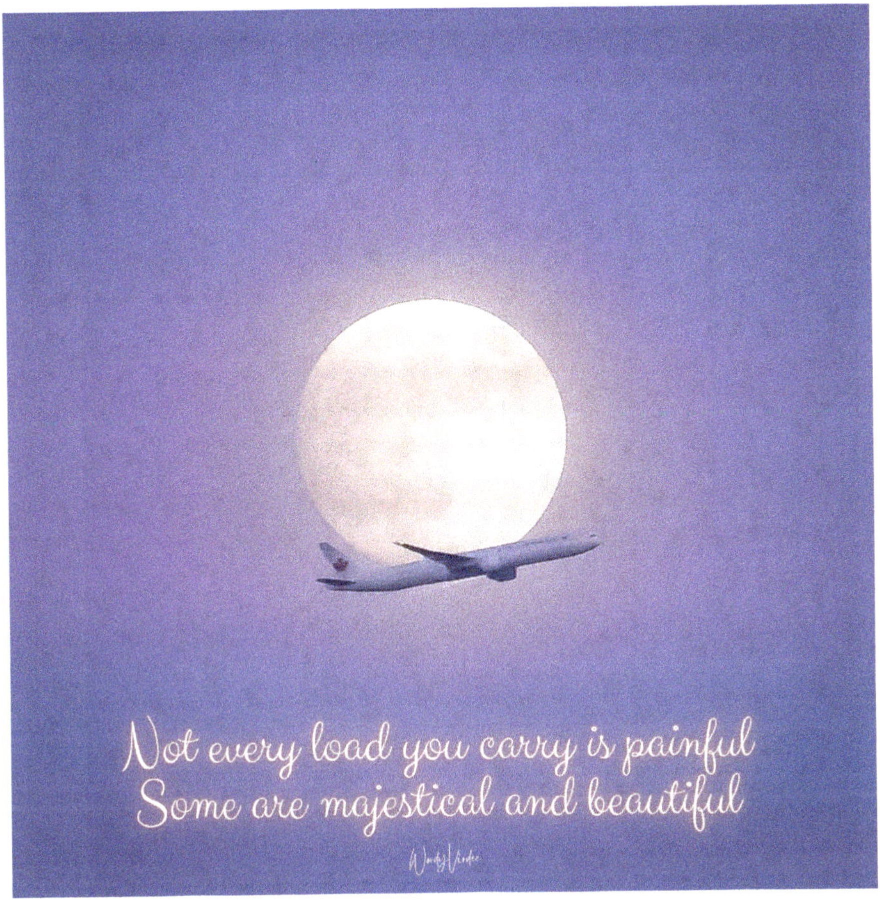

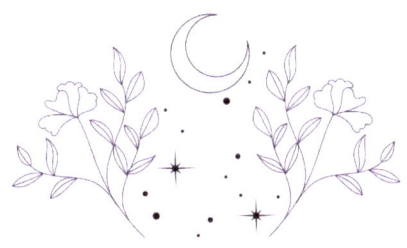

Not every load you carry is painful
Some are majestical and beautiful

The moon is new tonight
Heavenly sliver at a height
Oh! What a sight; the light;
A magnificent good night!

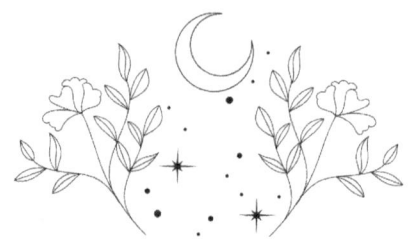

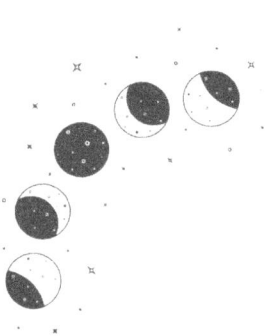

The moon is new tonight,
Heavenly sliver at a height.
Oh! What a sight; the light;
A magnificent good night!

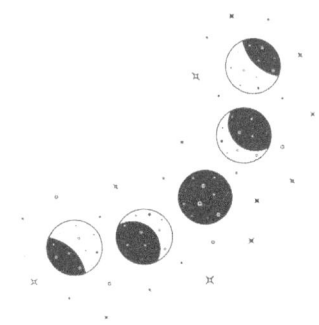

The warm wearisome day wore on,
Lingering heat from the sun trapped,
Within all dwellings, seeking way out,
Skylight dulled a little, breeze ensued,
The air within my room, chilled a little,
So did I, as the eye caught a glimpse,
Of the moon, so full and bright, rose,
Over the horizon, shifting hues from,
Warm colours to cooler shades of blue,
The moon gained more height, rising,
Brighter, raising spirits ever so higher.

The warm wearisome day wore on,
Lingering heat from the sun trapped,
Within all dwellings, seeking way out,
Skylight dulled a little, breeze ensued,
The air within my room, chilled a little,
So did I, as the eye caught a glimpse,
Of the moon, so full and bright, rose,
Over the horizon, shifting hues from,
Warm colours to cooler shades of blue,
The moon gained more height, rising,
Brighter, raising spirits ever so higher.

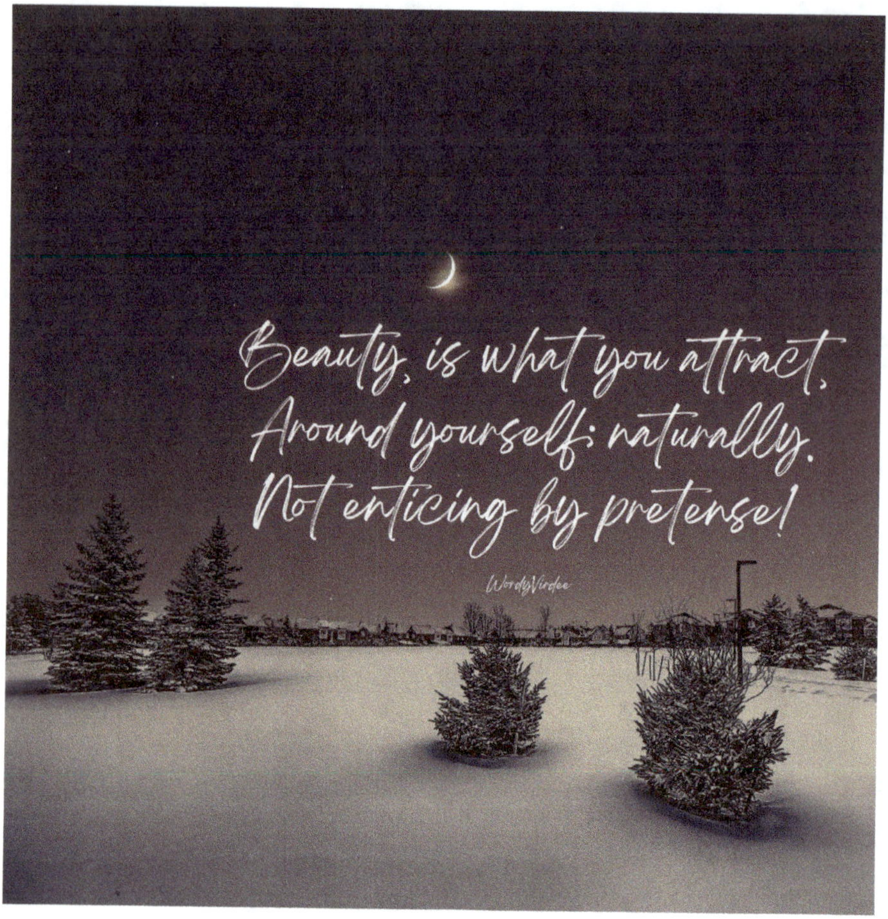

Beauty, is what you attract,
Around yourself; naturally.
Not enticing by pretense!

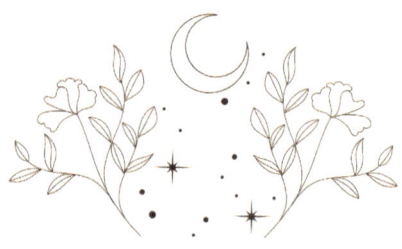

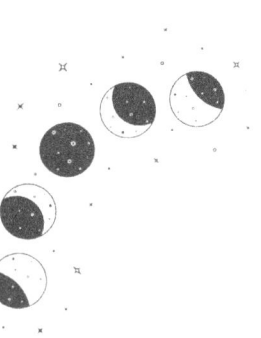

Beauty, is what you attract,
Around yourself; naturally.
Not enticing by pretense!

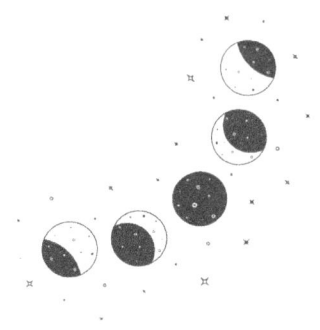

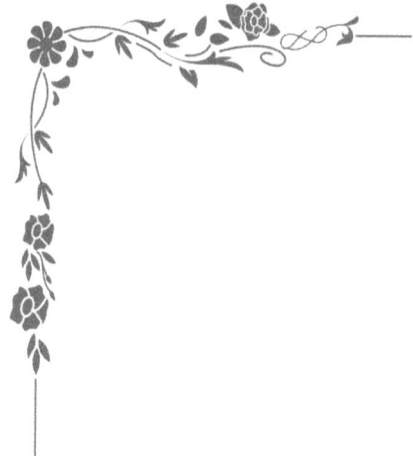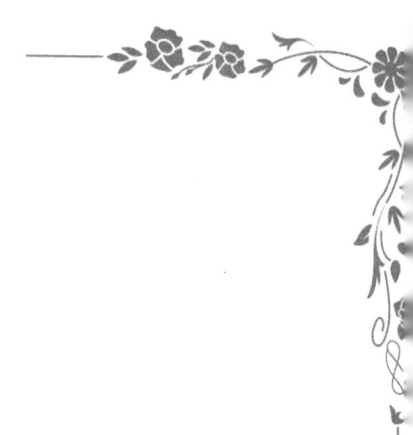

A cardinal sings sweet,
A spring song, a treat.
Pleasant wind carrying,
The melody so pleasing.
The gentle breeze blows,
Commending the compose.
Performance, simply adore,
Ears crave, forever more!

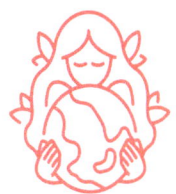

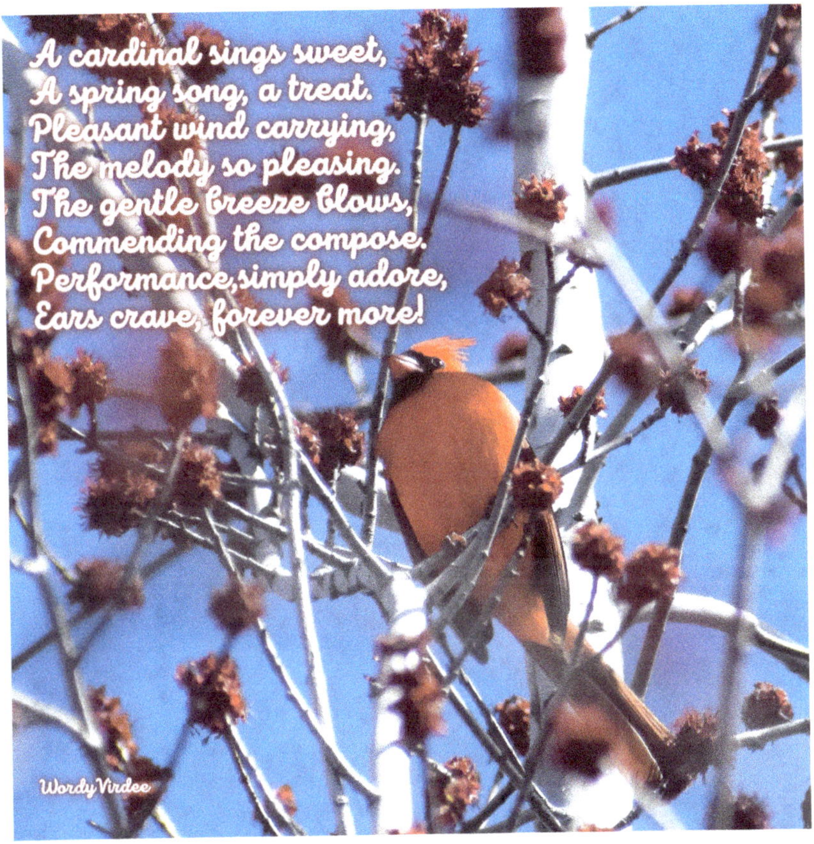

A cardinal sings sweet,
A spring song, a treat.
Pleasant wind carrying,
The melody so pleasing.
The gentle breeze blows,
Commending the compose.
Performance, simply adore,
Ears crave, forever more!

WordyVirdee

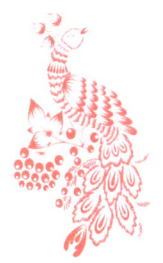

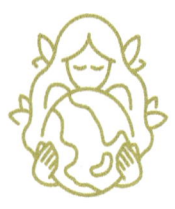

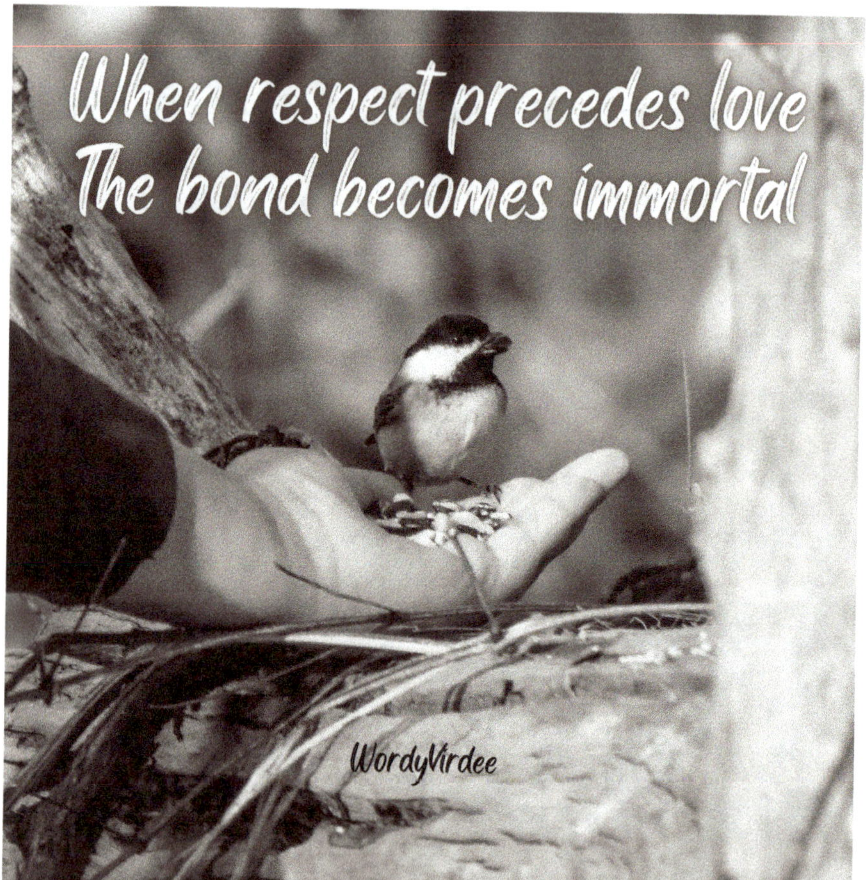

> When respect precedes love
> The bond becomes immortal
>
> WordyVirdee

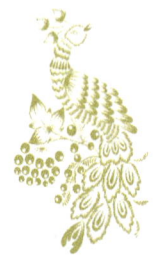

When respect precedes love,
The bond becomes immortal.

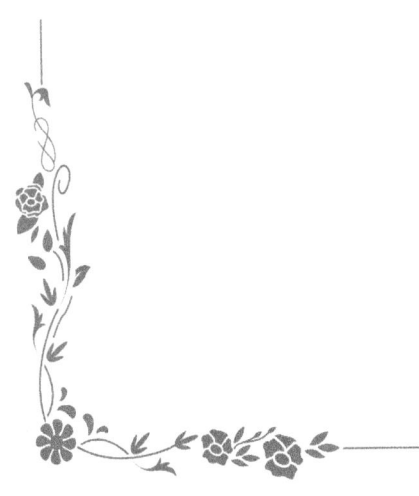

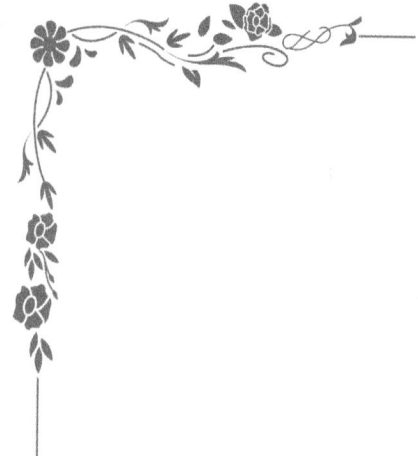

Let the pain you endure;
Define you, refine you,
Align you, design you.
Elevate you, to level up.
But, learn to let it not,
Confine you, malign you.
To hamper your cure!

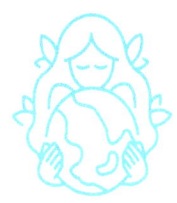

Let the pain you endure;
Define you, refine you,
Align you, design you.
Elevate you, to level up.

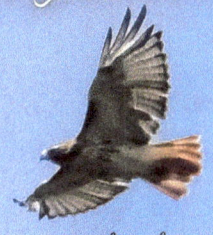

Wordy Virdee

But, learn to let it not,
Confine you, malign you.
To hamper your cure!

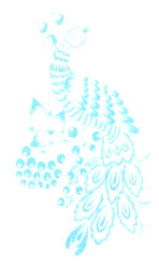

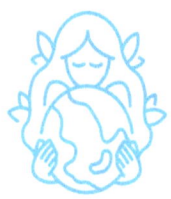

A few words inspired and penned in haste
Observing a bird across the sky as it raced
Life moments cherished, naturally graced

WordyVirdee

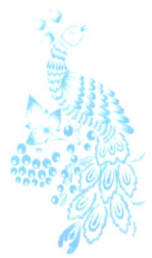

A few words inspired and penned in haste
Observing a bird across the sky as it raced
Life moments cherished, naturally graced

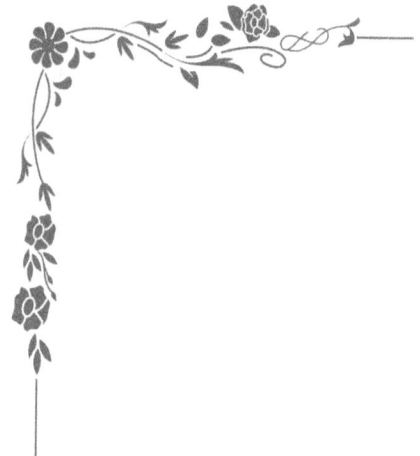

There'd be no reverance,
For the beauty of the moon,
Without utter darkness of sky.
To be distinguishable, to standout,
There needs to be a contradiction,
The pure whiteness of a swan is,
Insignificant for lack of contrast.
Seek the darkest parts deep within,
To illuminate that darkness beautifully.

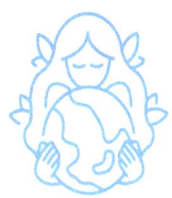

There'd be no reverance,
For the beauty of the moon,
Without utter darkness of sky.
To be distinguishable, to standout,
There needs to be a contradiction,
The pure whiteness of a swan is,
Insignificant for lack of contrast.
Seek the darkest parts deep within,
To illuminate that darkness beautifully.

Wordy Virdee

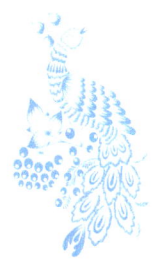

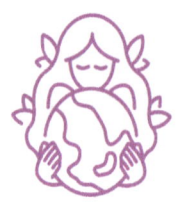

It was a crisp, bright shiny day,
Birds chirping extra, first of May.
Bees danced, the flowers sway,
Wind sang, so the trees could play,
Magical times, I joyfully must say.
I held her close, in my arms she lay,
Her eyes charming, can't look away.
A proud father, my first born, oh yay!
Wish she is forever blessed, I pray!

Wordy Virdee

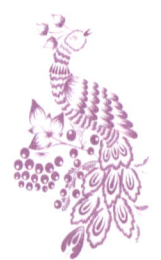

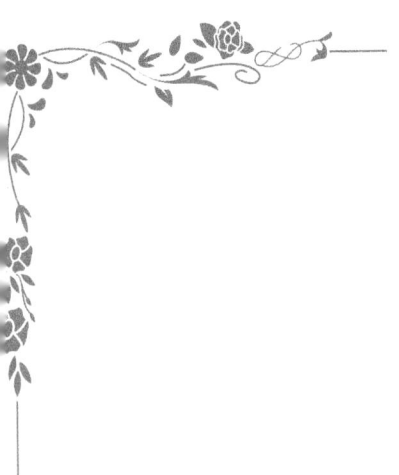
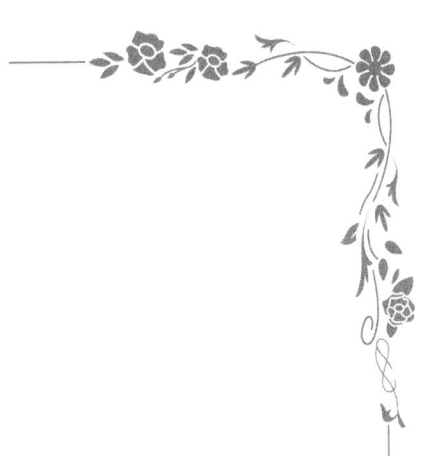

It was a crisp, bright shiny day,
Birds chirping extra, first of May.
Bees danced, the flowers sway,
Wind sang, so the trees could play,
Magical times, I joyfully must say.
I held her close, in my arms she lay,
Her eyes charming, can't look away.
A proud father, my first born, oh yay!
Wish she is forever blessed, I pray!

Trek solely through the forest
Rejuvenating your mind and soul

For it's extremely fatigued from
Unnecessary, baseless daily efforts

Superficial, shallow worthless links
Poisoning conscience, draining energy

Thus, make haste into the woods, where
Streams flow, flowers bloom, bees buzz

Birds tweet and sing, crickets cheep and
Chirp, duly replenishing your essence

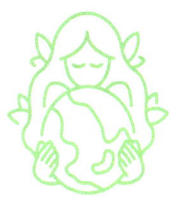

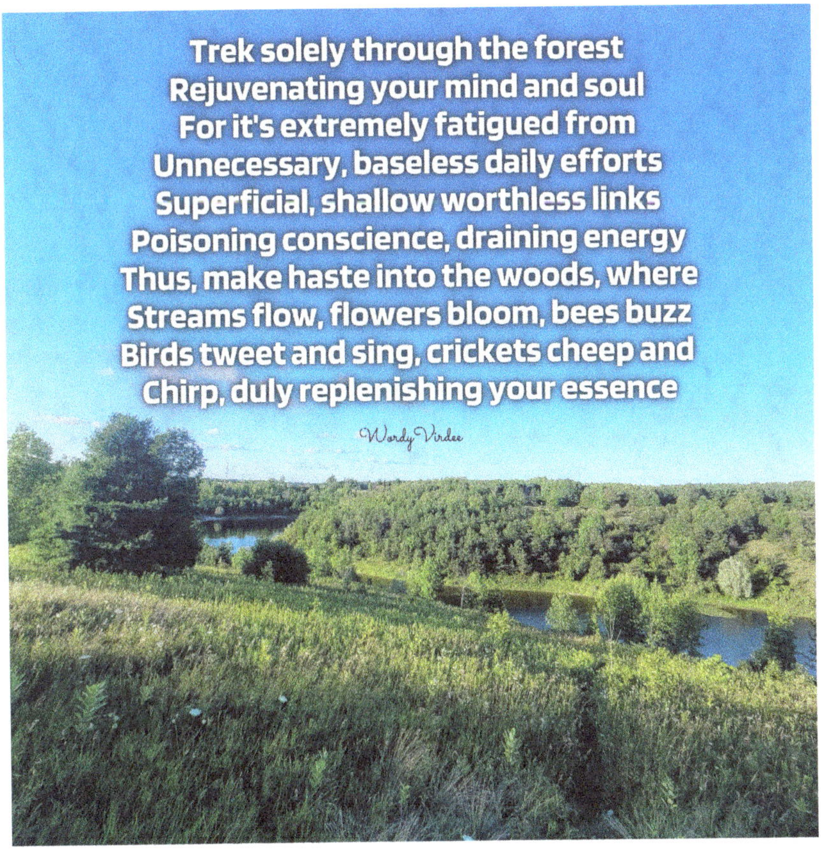

Trek solely through the forest
Rejuvenating your mind and soul
For it's extremely fatigued from
Unnecessary, baseless daily efforts
Superficial, shallow worthless links
Poisoning conscience, draining energy
Thus, make haste into the woods, where
Streams flow, flowers bloom, bees buzz
Birds tweet and sing, crickets cheep and
Chirp, duly replenishing your essence

Wordy Virdee

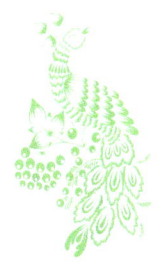

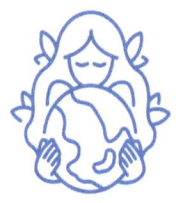

Your breath ignites your soul,
Burning thy flame nicely aglow.
Why waste your precious fuel,
Arresting you from your growth?
Cherish your moments; whole,
Life do not, cheaply you throw.
Rise, elevate, set yourself a goal,
Progress, no matter how slow!

WordyVirdee

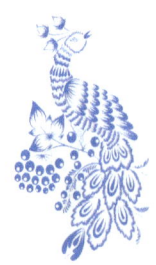

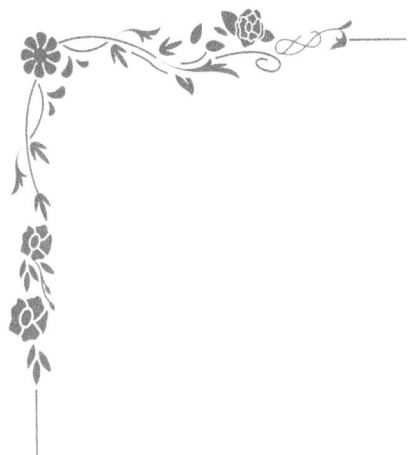

Your breath ignites your soul,
Burning thy flame nicely aglow.
Why waste your precious fuel,
Arresting you from your growth?
Cherish your moments; whole,
Life do not, cheaply you throw.
Rise, elevate, set yourself a goal,
Progress, no matter how slow!

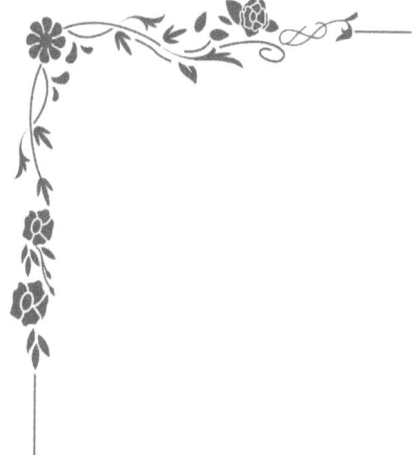

Soul imbued in colours of nature
Intrinsic hues, a fine nomenclature
Each moment, a divine portraiture!

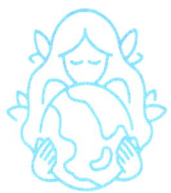

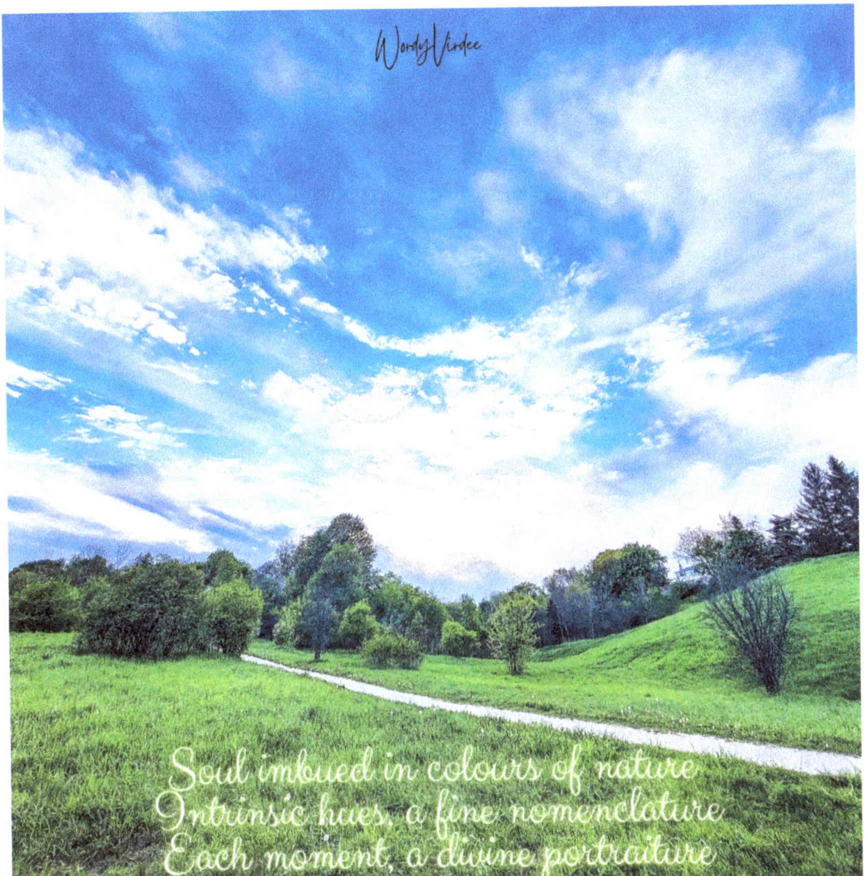

Soul imbued in colours of nature
Intrinsic hues, a fine nomenclature
Each moment, a divine portraiture

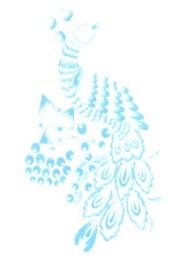

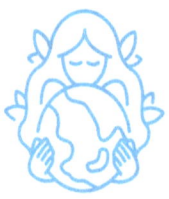

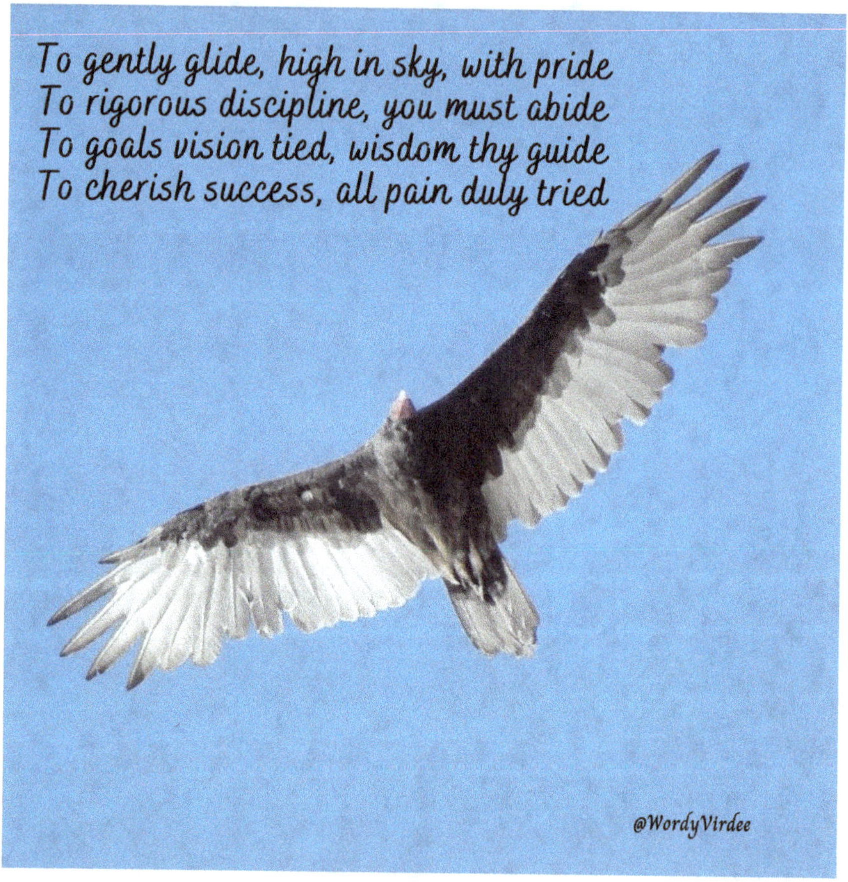

To gently glide, high in sky, with pride
To rigorous discipline, you must abide
To goals vision tied, wisdom thy guide
To cherish success, all pain duly tried

@WordyVirdee

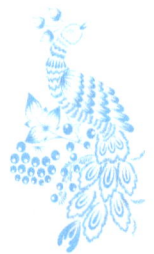

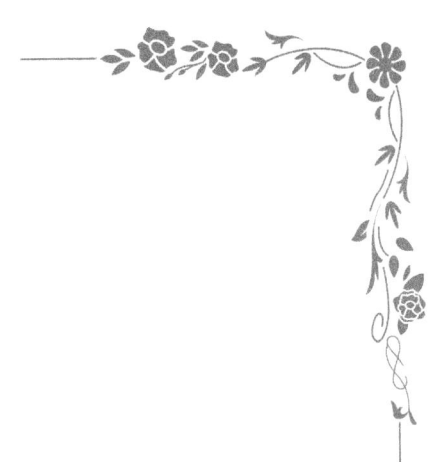

To gently glide, high in sky, with pride
To rigorous discipline, you must abide
To goals vision tied, wisdom thy guide
To cherish success, all pain duly tried

You're extremely beautiful
When you burn. Like a star,
Sun burns and glows hot,
It gives shine to the moon!
Without that light, Venus
Has no existence of it's own.
Wouldn't see Jupiter or Mars
Exist in their majestic glory!
So burn and shine like a star!
Be the star, sprinkle stardust
On all within your reach, all
That see you. Endure the heat,
Flare bright; Burn and shine!
Feed flowers, radiate warmth,
Let the colours in petals vividly
Shimmer through pleasantly!
Attracting butterflies and bees,
Flirting and caressing in the wind,
Dancing around buds and radiance,
Giving love a meaning that's divine.

You're extremely beautiful
When you burn. Like a star,
Sun burns and glows hot,
It gives shine to the moon!
Without that light, Venus
Has no existence of it's own.
Wouldn't see Jupiter or Mars
Exist in their majestic glory!
So burn and shine like a star!
Be the star, sprinkle stardust
On all within your reach, all
That see you. Endure the heat,
Flare bright; Burn and shine!
Feed flowers, radiate warmth,
Let the colours in petals vividly
Shimmer through pleasantly!
Attracting butterflies and bees,
Flirting and caressing in the wind,
Dancing around buds and radiance,
Giving love a meaning that's divine.

Wordy Virdee

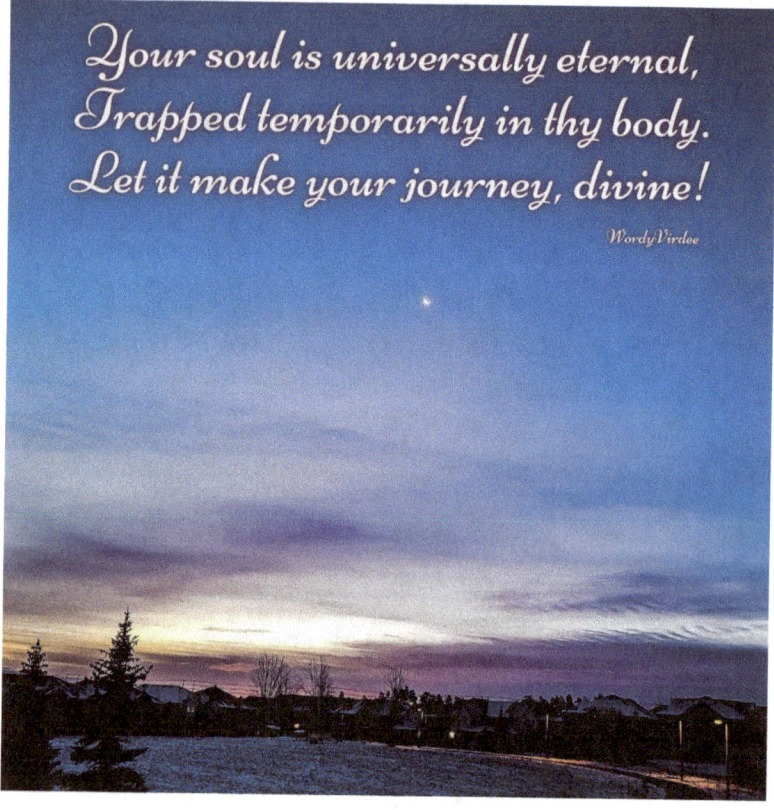

Your soul is universally eternal,
Trapped temporarily in thy body.
Let it make your journey, divine!.

We all feel it from time to time,
In various forms, in many ways.
It rolls down cheeks as tear drops,
It metaphorically, maims heartbeats.
It's PAIN I'm referring to, of loss, grief,
From rejection, desolation, dejection.
It disguises in veils but feels the same,
Physical scars treat, quicker even, better.
But mental scars cut deep, always hidden,
Carried deep within our souls in heaps.
Let us carry our burdens, assist others,
The best we can, pain divided after all,
Shared equally; how as humans, we heal.

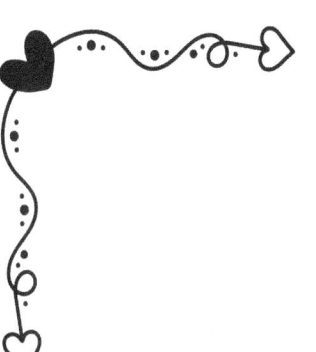
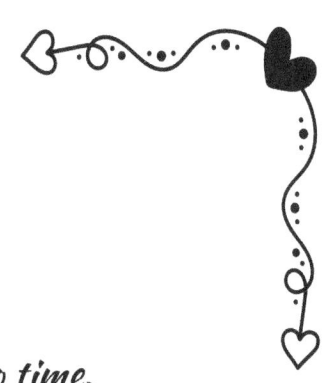

We all feel it from time to time,
In various forms, in many ways.
It rolls down cheeks, as tear drops,
It metaphorically, maims heartbeats.
It's PAIN I'm referring to; of loss, grief,
From rejection, desolation, dejection.
It disguises in veils, but feels the same,
Physical scars treat, quicker even, better.
But mental scars cut deep, always hidden,
Carried deep within our souls in heaps.
Let us carry our burdens, assist others,
The best we can, pain divided after all,
Shared equally; how as humans, we heal.

Wordy Virdee

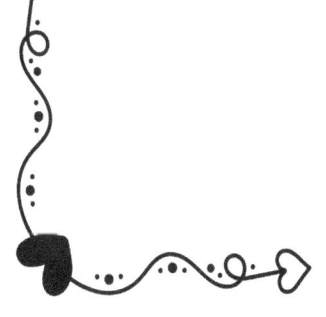

WordsVerlee

A poet is someone enthralling, who,
Talks with, when you read in your silence.
Sharing your magical, wonderful love story.
Walks with you, matching your strides,
While you stroll through your mind in bed.
Sings with you, crooning to your lovely tune,
A love song written, touching your bare soul.
Dances with you, when you cherish those
Memories, words resonating the musical beat.
Kisses your parted lips, as you read those rhymes,
Engraved on your heart, a mystical secret entry code.
That's a poet, for you, keeping you forever on your toes.

A poet is someone enthralling, who,
Talks with, when you read in your silence.
Sharing your magical, wonderful love story.
Walks with you, matching your strides,
While you stroll through your mind in bed.
Sings with you, crooning to your lovely tune,
A love song written, touching your bare soul.
Dances with you, when you cherish those,
Memories, words resonating the musical beat.
Kisses your parted lips, as you read those rhymes,
Engraved on your heart, a mystical secret entry code.
That's a poet, for you, keeping you forever on your toes.

From the moment we are conceived,
As the heart begins to pump and beat,
The cells replicate, multiply and grow.
It's a constant battle, tussle of survival,
To leave the confines of mother's womb,
Into an awaiting world, full of challenges.
First breath of oxygen, piercing the lungs,
Effecting a snivel, a fine taste of reception,
Of life at play, for moments that lie in wait.
Must be a purpose, can't just be a crusade?
Some bonds formed by blood, others by love,
Some hearts mended by affection, some,
Shattered by same, what drama, what play!
Sentient beings, learned, above all critters,
Our purpose has to be more than mundane,
It's the power we harness, to make change.
A difference we can all make, to rise above,
For ourselves foremost, carving the way,
For others not to go astray, the plot of play!
Making a difference on this world stage,
As the drama unfolds around us, everyday,
Keep show amusing, for everyone, in every way!

From the moment we are conceived,
As the heart begins to pump and beat,
The cells replicate, multiply and grow.
It's a constant battle, tussle of survival,
To leave the confines of mother's womb,
Into an awaiting world, full of challenges.
First breath of oxygen, piercing the lungs,
Effecting a snivel, a fine taste of reception,
Of life at play, for moments that lie in wait.
Must be a purpose, can't just be a crusade?
Some bonds formed by blood, others by love,
Some hearts mended by affection, some,
Shattered by same, what drama, what play!
Sentient beings, learned, above all critters,
Our purpose has to be more than mundane,
It's the power we harness, to make change.
A difference we can all make, to rise above,
For ourselves foremost, carving the way,
For others not to go astray, the plot of play!
Making a difference on this world stage,
As the drama unfolds around us, everyday,
Keep show amusing, for everyone, in every way!

WordyVirdee

The tragic demise of modern Humanity is, we've normalized Acceptance of virtues as an old Fashioned, terrible way of life!

WordyVirdee

The tragic demise of modern
Humanity is, we've normalized
Acceptance of virtues as an old
Fashioned, terrible way of life!

Discover paths for journeys most travelled
Those are least frequented and unravelled
Seek joy & peace, mind endlessly bedazzled
For common routes have everyone frazzled

Discover paths for journeys most travelled
Those are least frequented and unravelled
Seek joy & peace, mind endlessly bedazzled
For common routes have everyone frazzled

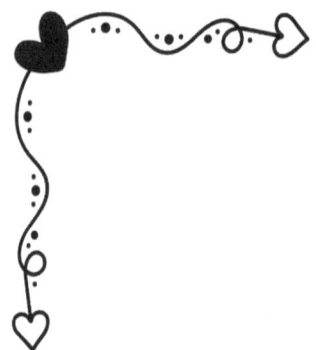
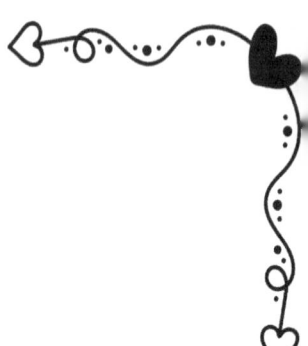

How strange is this heart
Gentle and light when filled
By beloved's affectionate start
Stabbed, slashed, fallen from grace
Squeezed mercilessly by sweetheart
Heavier it felt, as emptier it got
Draining painfully, dripping apart

Wordy Virdee

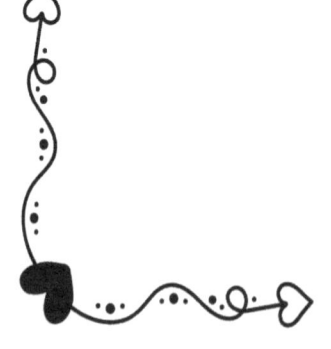
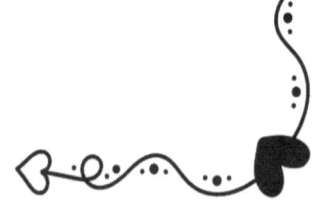

How strange is this heart
Gentle and light when filled
By beloved's affectionate start
Stabbed, slashed, fallen from grace
Squeezed mercilessly by sweetheart
Heavier it felt, as emptier it got
Draining painfully, dripping apart

We, unfortunately, live in a world
Where we have to constantly fight
For peace of mind and happiness
Battle that must be won individually
Commanded duly by thy power of will
Commanding your ever wavering mind
To conjure up army of courage within
Standing guard against raging vices
Relentless attacks weakening emotions
In essence constant everlasting combat
Victory savoured by a mind fully in control

We, unfortunately, live in a world
Where we have to constantly fight
For peace of mind and happiness
Battle that must be won individually
Commanded duly by thy power of will
Commanding your ever wavering mind
To conjure up army of courage within
Standing guard against raging vices
Relentless attacks weakening emotions
In essence constant everlasting combat
Victory savoured by a mind fully in control

@WordyVirdee

That pure earthly smell as droplets strike
Clouds heavy and dark, rolling it feels like
A little child erratically pedalling a trike
The birds chirping away playful childlike
Winds flirting with trees, all smitten alike
Signs of Spring at last, nature's best psych

That pure earthly smell as droplets strike
Clouds heavy and dark, rolling it feels like
A little child erratically pedalling a trike
The birds chirping away playful childlike
Winds flirting with trees, all smitten alike
Signs of Spring at last, nature's best psych

Each one of us desire to fly back in time
Yearning sweet memories to forever shine
Soul illumined brightly, sparkling sublime
Gloom eternally dispersed all through showtime
Of life, for everlasting joyous staged mime

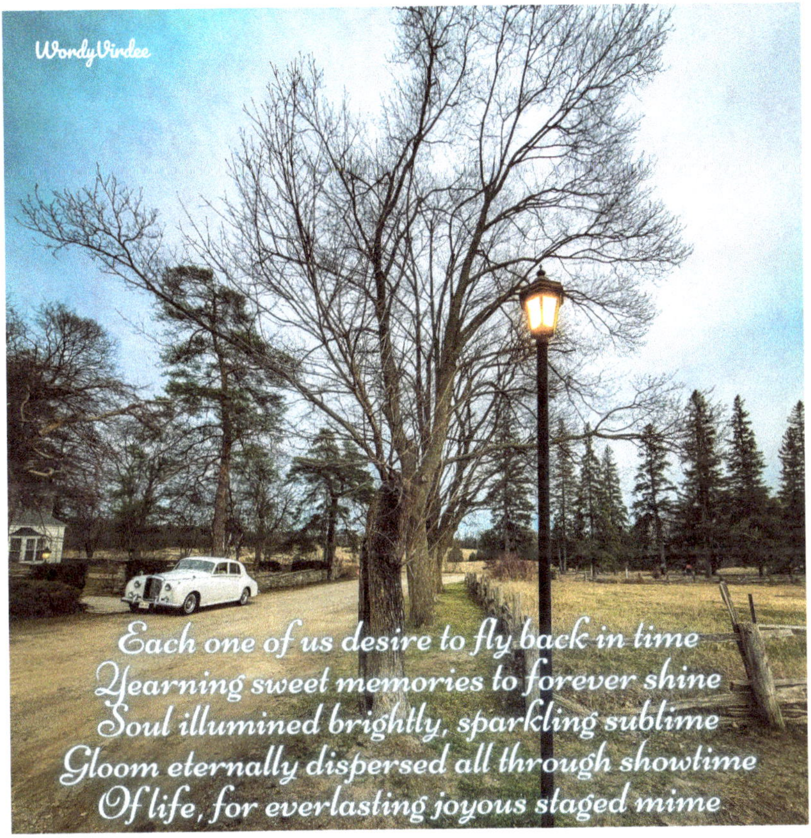

Each one of us desire to fly back in time
Yearning sweet memories to forever shine
Soul illumined brightly, sparkling sublime
Gloom eternally dispersed all through showtime
Of life, for everlasting joyous staged mime

Here and now, float like a bubble
Joys and pain, within as you juggle
In a blink, it pops, all down to rubble

Wordy Virdee

Here and now, float like a bubble
Joys and pain, within as you juggle
In a blink, it pops, all down to rubble

Do not despair
We're all incomplete

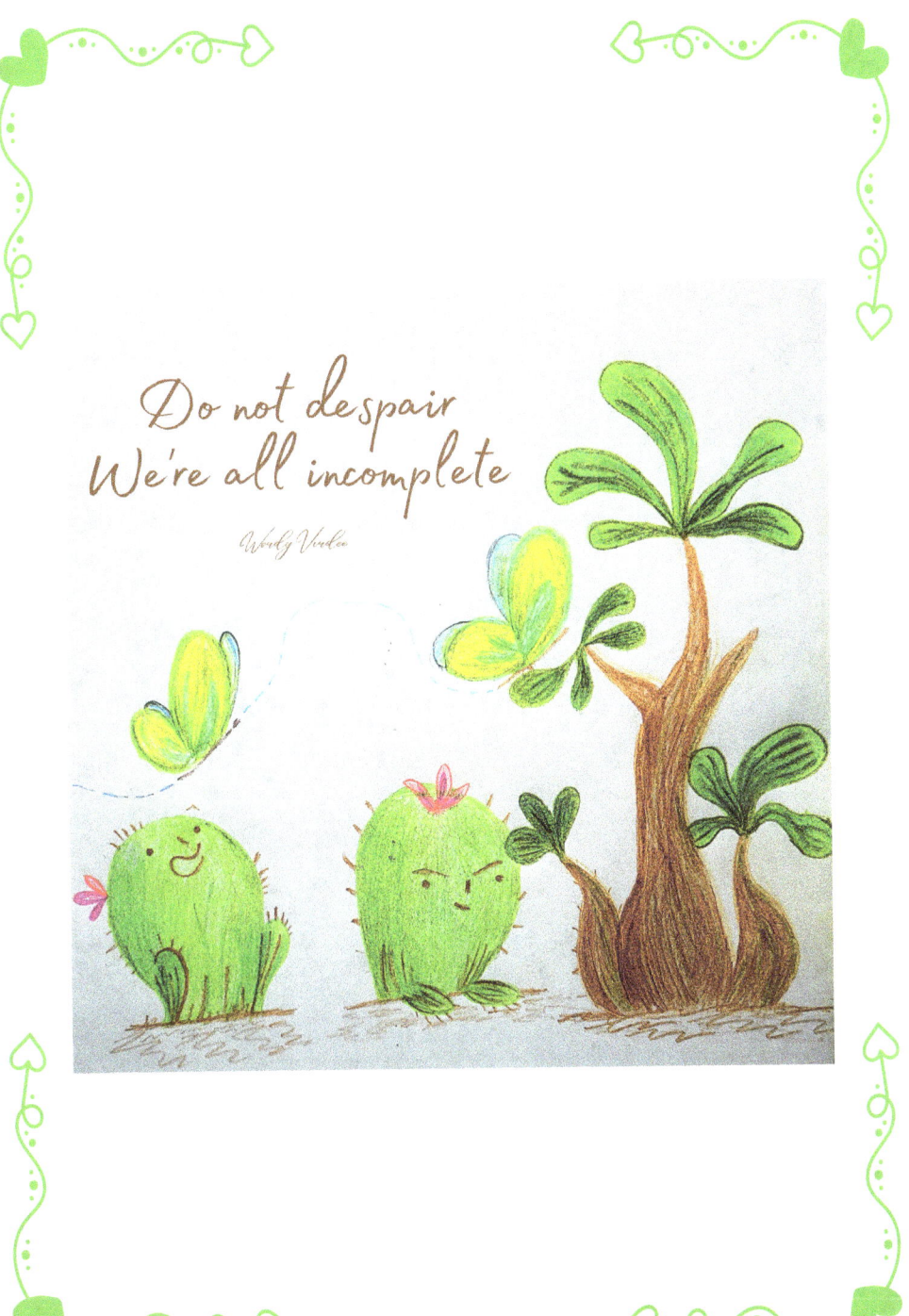

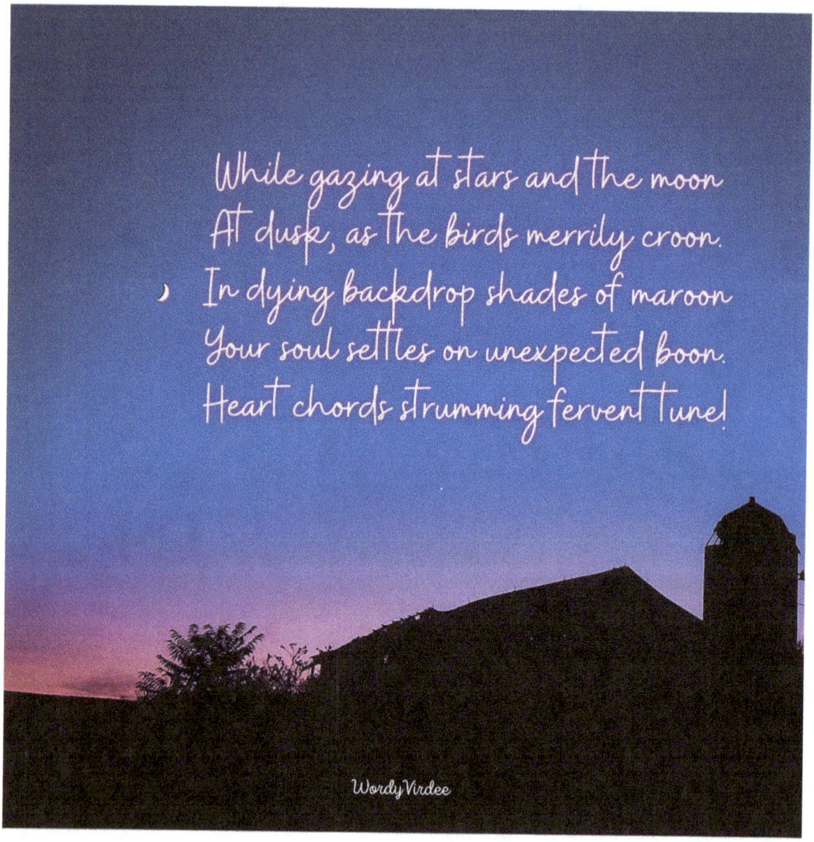

While gazing at stars and the moon
At dusk, as the birds merrily croon.
In dying backdrop shades of maroon
Your soul settles on unexpected boon.
Heart chords strumming fervent tune!

WordyVirdee

While gazing at stars and the moon
At dusk, as the birds merrily croon.
In dying backdrop shades of maroon
Your soul settles on unexpected boon.
Heart chords strumming fervent tune!

The one & only factor
In the way of 'sacred'
And you being 'scared'
Is the shift of letter 'c'.
'C'ourage is all it takes!
'C'onquer all your fears!
'C'laim your blessings!

The one & only factor
In the way of 'sacred'
And you being 'scared'
Is the shift of letter 'c'.
'C'ourage is all it takes!
'C'onquer all your fears!
'C'laim your blessings!

WordyWirdee

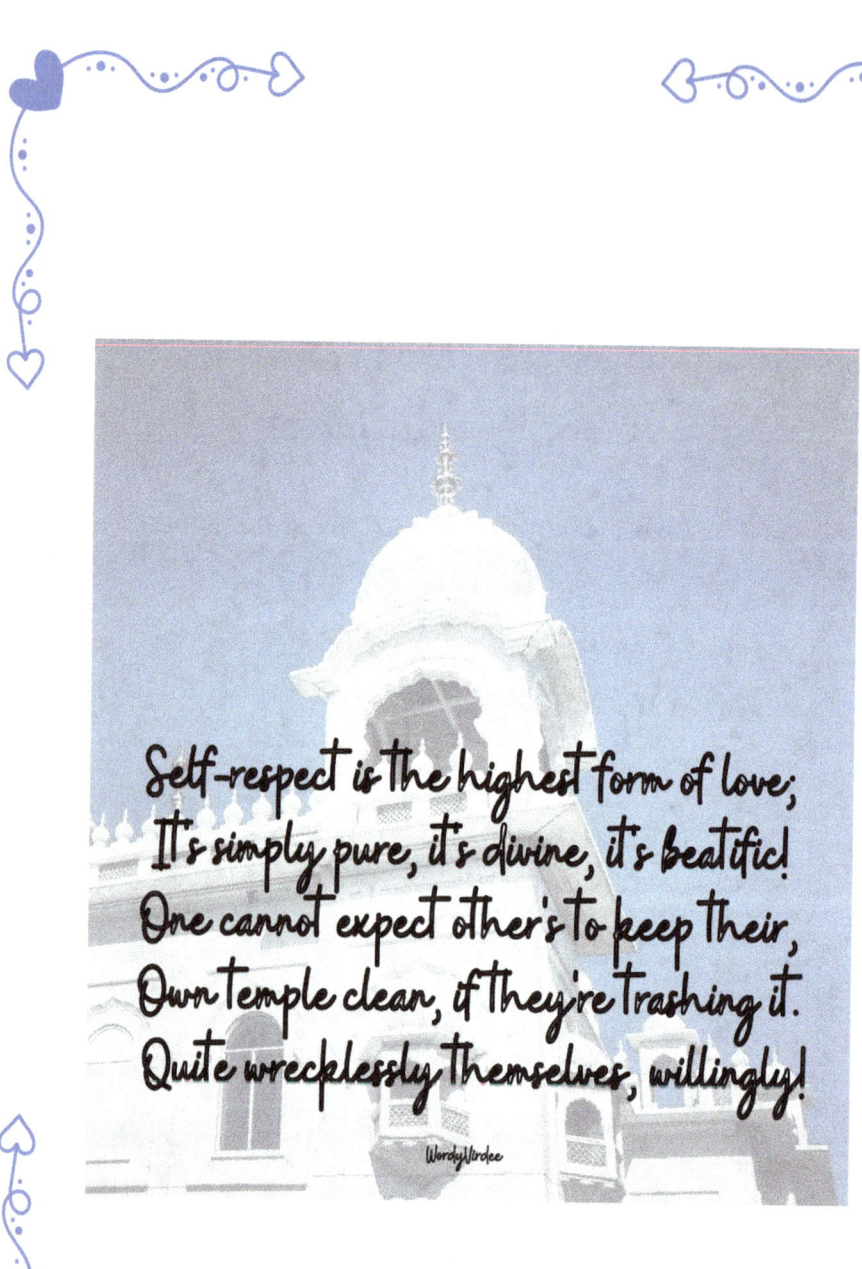

Self-respect is the highest form of love;
It's simply pure, it's divine, it's beatific!
One cannot expect other's to keep their,
Own temple clean, if they're trashing it.
Quite wrecklessly themselves, willingly!

In this world gone astray.
I humbly, sincerely pray.
May ever, not anyone slay.
Another being, on any day.
Resolve conflicts; tell, say.
Liaise, words openly all lay.
To honestly and fairly, play.
So peace can forever stay.
Hope my prayer can sway.
World towards peaceful way

In this world gone astray,
I humbly, sincerely pray,
May ever, not anyone slay,
Another being, on any day,
Resolve conflicts tell, say,
Liaise, words openly all lay,
To honestly and fairly, play,
So peace can forever stay,
Hope my prayer can sway,
World towards peaceful way.

WordyVirdee

Early morning autumnal rain,
Tapping gently on my window.
Broke my slumber, scrubbing
My dream, where I was merrily
Dancing in summer monsoon.
On sandy desert dunes crafted
Ever so elegantly by blazing wind.
The striking raindrop sound on the
Glass, synchronized with rhythm
Of each swaying step, as my trance
Waned, from the soft wet sand under
My bare feet, to the coziness of my
Beloved. Keep tapping rapturous rain!

Wordy Virdee

Early morning autumnal rain,
Tapping gently on my window.
Broke my slumber, scrubbing
My dream, where I was merrily
Dancing in summer monsoon.
On sandy desert dunes crafted
Ever so elegantly by blazing wind.
The striking raindrop sound on the
Glass, synchronized with rhythm
Of each swaying step, as my trance
Waned, from the soft wet sand under
My bare feet, to the coziness of my
Beloved. Keep tapping rapturous rain.

www.ingramcontent.com/pod-product-compliance
Lightning Source LLC
Chambersburg PA
CBHW070252220526
45465CB00004B/1598